GREAT PAINTERS

PIERO VENTURA

GREAT PAINTERS

G. P. PUTNAM'S SONS   NEW YORK

The author wishes to thank Roberto Pasini for collaborating on the text and preparing the biographies of the painters, and his son Marco Ventura for helping with the coloring of the drawings. Special thanks to Margherita Forestan for her friendly assistance in researching and collecting the photographic material.

Copyright © 1984 by Arnoldo Mondadori Editore S.p.A., Milano
English translation copyright © 1984
by Arnoldo Mondadori Editore S.p.A., Milano
Originally published in Italy by Arnoldo Mondadori Editore, 1983, under the title *I Grandi Pittori*
English translation by Geoffrey Culverwell
Translation adapted by Judith St. George
Printed and bound in Spain by Artes Graficas Toledo S.A.
First Impression
Book design by Mike Suh

Library of Congress Cataloging in Publication Data
Ventura, Piero. / Great painters.
    Translation of: I Grandi pittori. / Includes index.
    1. Painters—Biography. I. Title.
ND35.V34 1984 759 [B] 84-3423
ISBN 0-399-21115-2
D. L. TO: 667-1984

CONTENTS

Introduction

Who was the first great painter in history? Where was he born? What did he paint?

We will never know. We don't know the first great painter or the thousands of painters who followed. They never recorded their names on their works and, besides, very few of their works have survived.

Only two painters' names have come down to us from ancient Greece, Polygnotus and Apelles, although even these artists are more legend than historical fact since none of their paintings still exist. Strangely enough, many great sculptors from the same period of Greek history, such as Phidias and Praxiteles, are known to us. Perhaps their names endured because their sculptures have survived. Or perhaps the ancient Greeks preferred sculpture to paintings, or considered sculpture more important. Certainly it was more durable. Whatever the reason, it wasn't until the 13th century that we find a painting that bears the name of its artist.

Nevertheless, man began to create images of what he saw around him as early as ten to fifteen thousand years ago, when our ancestors painted beautiful and mysterious pictures in caves and on rock-faces around the world that can still be seen today. The first professional painters emerged in the great civilizations of Sumeria and Egypt. Images covered the mosaics of Ur, the walls and gates of Babylon, the Palace of Darius at Susa, the Royal Palace of Mari, the Pharaohs' temples. Even the Egyptian writing known as hieroglyphics recalls a period of great artistic activity.

Decorated wth mythical figures dancing around a temple, this Greek vase, known as an amphora, dates around 490 B.C. The vase is made of red clay and has been painted with black paint up to the edges of the figures. The figures are the red clay left unpainted. The detail of their costumes is painted on with black paint.

Household goods such as plates, vases and amphoras from ancient Greece reveal great painting skill. Often using a single color, black, against the reddish-brown background of the baked clay or terracotta from which their pottery was made, Greek painters illustrated the myths of their history and religion with ability and elegance.

Because the figures on Greek pottery were baked permanently into the surface during the manufacturing process, they have survived in good condition. Unfortunately, because paintings on wood or on walls cannot be baked, many have been lost. The painters of classical antiquity tried to preserve paintings for a longer time and invented encaustic painting, a process which involved heat. They mixed their colors with boiling wax, resin and vegetable oils. Although this procedure was widely used during Roman times, its exact formula has since been lost.

This is one of a series of paintings that covered the walls of the impressive banquet or reception room in the Villa of the Mysteries at Pompeii. You can see how realistic painting looked in Roman times (about 60 B.C.). Here a pregnant lady is bringing a plate of cakes to a table.

This mosaic, in the church of San Vitale at Ravenna, Italy, was made in A.D. 530–550. It shows Theodora, Empress of Byzantium, with two bishops and her court of ladies. She is offering a gift to the Church. The mosaic is high up on a wall beside the altar of the church.

Because wealthy Roman citizens were fond of art, fresco paintings covered the walls of their houses with landscapes, still lifes and animals, as well as religious and historical subjects. Although the Roman painters were technically skillful, very few of their works have endured.

With the decline of the Roman Empire, the Romans' artistic heritage was taken over by the Byzantines. The ancient city of Byzantium, renamed Constantinople in A.D. 330 as the new capital of the Roman Empire, became the new center for artists. The main interest of the Romanized Greeks of Byzantium was mosaic-making, an art form which involved setting small squares of glass or colored stone into cement to make a pattern. It was a technique which the Romans had used primarily to decorate the floors of their houses.

Unlike the realism of Roman painting, the figures on Byzantine mosaics had elongated faces and strange gestures, and appeared not to have flesh-and-blood bodies under their long robes. These sophisticated and intellectual, but still nameless artists, did not seem concerned with portraying physical reality.

Giotto and the New Art

In a small village in the Mugello mountains of Italy, not far from the city of Florence, Giotto di Bondone was born in 1266 or 1267. Although almost nothing is known about his early years, there is a story that the famous painter Cimabue was passing through the region when he noticed a shepherd boy sketching the head of a goat on a rock. He was so impressed by the boy's obvious talent that he offered to teach him how to paint in his own workshop in nearby Florence.

This is Vespignano, the hill-village where Giotto was born.

Giotto, newly arrived in Florence, asks the way to Cimabue's studio.

This may not have happened at all, but it is known that Giotto left his village when he was about fifteen and moved to Florence so that he could learn a craft. At that time Florence was a rich and important city, chiefly because of its wool trade, and Giotto's father wanted his son to become a wool worker. However, Giotto spent so much time in Cimabue's workshop, his father finally relented and allowed him to stay there and learn to paint.

Giotto worked for several years in Cimabue's workshop, first as an apprentice and then as an assistant. During that time he would have seen many of his master's works, including the great *Crucifix*, a solemn painting filled with tragedy and suffering.

In his upper-level workshop, Cimabue and his young apprentices are constructing a large wooden cross that they will later paint and gild. Apprentices work and board in their master's house for years, their only pay the secrets of their master's craft. On the ground floor, Cimabue's wife and her maids prepare a meal.

Most of the commissions that came to painters in those days were from churches and convents. Although city councils, as well as rich citizens, also commissioned paintings, the paintings were usually presented to churches as gifts. Consequently, the subjects were always religious, and the paintings became an effective medium for explaining the life of Christ and the saints to the faithful, most of whom could neither read nor write.

During the same period, another great painter, Duccio di Buoninsegna, was at work in Siena. Although he too was influenced by Cimabue, he not only had a more gentle style, but he also placed a greater emphasis on the shape of his figures. Siena was only a day's journey by horseback from Florence, so perhaps Giotto was present when Duccio's great wooden panel painting of the *Maestà* was carried in a procession from his studio to the Cathedral. Because it had taken Duccio four years to complete the work, the impressive procession seemed almost like a celebration of the art of painting itself.

This picture by Duccio of the Virgin Mary seated on glittering gold and surrounded by saints and angels is known as the Maestà, which means "majesty," a fitting title.

When Giotto was about thirty years old, Franciscan monks invited him to come to Assisi. St. Francis of Assisi, whose message had made a profound impact on the religious life of the period, had died there only seventy years before. The order of Franciscan monks he had founded had spread rapidly, and now the head of the order wanted Giotto to paint frescoes on the walls of the new church that had been built in St. Francis's honor. As was customary at the time, the monks gave Giotto exact instructions as to which episodes of St. Francis's life and works they wanted him to portray.

This church is called the Upper Church of St. Francis because it was built above the remains of an older one, also dedicated to St. Francis. Giotto seems overwhelmed at the sight of all these walls just waiting for his decorations.

Giotto, working here on the walls with his apprentices, has already finished three scenes from the life of St. Francis: The Homage of a Simple Man (left), The Saint Gives Away His Cloak (center), and The Renunciation of Worldly Goods (right).

In those days it was traditional for artists to depict saints and members of the Holy Family in a certain position, wearing certain clothes and seated in the correct place so they could always be recognized by the congregation. Both Cimabue's *Crucifix* and Duccio's *Maestà*, for example, look more like Byzantine mosaics than real people. But Giotto set out to paint what he saw with his eyes, and used the faces of ordinary people from the streets of Assisi for his figures. He even used a model to portray St. Francis. His contemporaries were delighted with this "new art," and an artistic revolution was launched.

Painting the fresco **The Saint Preaches to the Birds** *involves many steps.*

The worker first chips the plaster with a hammer to roughen it, then dampens it with water.

He applies a new layer of plaster which he carefully smooths to make a completely flat surface.

On a large sheet of paper, the artist has already drawn the figures to be painted, making pinpricks around the outlines. This drawing, known as a cartoon, is first applied to the wall and then charcoal dust is blown through the pinpricks to transfer the outlines onto the plaster.

The artist joins up the dotted lines, either with a brush dipped in dark ink or with a pointed stick that makes a small groove.

The fresco is finished. Because the work has to be completed before the plaster dries, only enough fresh plaster is applied at a time for one day's painting.

17

Simone Martini sketches the castle for his painting of Guidoriccio da Fogliano, fifty years after the event.

Certain independent Italian cities that had grown rich and powerful wanted to celebrate their military and political successes in paintings. The people of Siena hired Simone Martini, one of Siena's greatest artists, to commemorate the capture of the castles of Montemassi and Sassoforte in the Maremma by their military leader, Guidoriccio da Fogliano. Because the fresco was to decorate a room in Siena's Palazzo Pubblico, the important Town Hall where the city's government was housed, Simone had to make sure that all his details were historically accurate.

Just like now, what an artist earned depended on his reputation and on how astute he was at running his business. The city paid Simone 16 florins for his frescoes. Considering that four years earlier, he had paid 20 florins for a fine house, his work brought him in a very good income indeed.

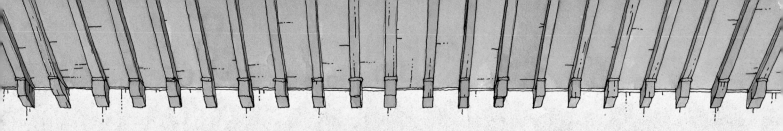

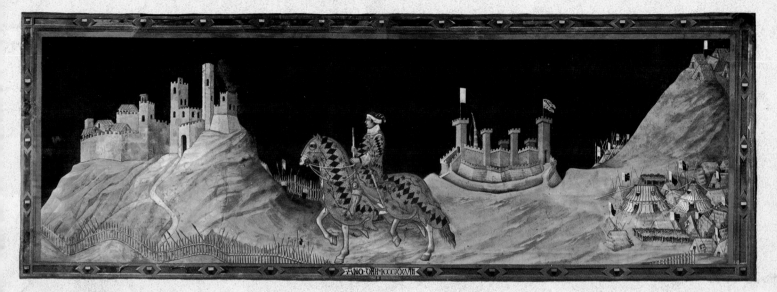

Simone's painting Guidoriccio da Fogliano *shows the castles that are being besieged, on the left. On the right, a temporary fortress is equipped with a launching device for stone missiles. Although the scene, including the encampment and the palisade, is historically accurate, there is a fairytale quality to it. The imaginative Simone, who was attracted to the world of chivalry, has portrayed the central figure, Guidoriccio, as a solitary knight rather than as a military leader. With the horse and rider elegantly clothed in the same richly decorated cloth, the mood is more of a jousting tournament or a court reception than a war.*

19

A Strange Partnership

Although Giotto's "new art," with its lively figures moving against realistic backgrounds, marked a turning point in the history of painting, for more than a century, many Italian painters still favored the courtly style of Simone. Gentile da Fabriano had such a style. In Italian, *gentile* means fine or noble and as Michelangelo himself remarked approvingly, never has an artist's name been so accurately described in his works as in the case of Gentile da Fabriano.

The priest of the church of Santa Trinità has just arrived to view Gentile's Adoration of the Magi. It is hard to imagine that anyone in the stable where Jesus was born would have worn the elegant clothes in which Gentile painted them. These are the clothes of the lords, cardinals and clients whom Gentile knew well.

Masolino is seen climbing toward Castiglione Olona, a small village in northern Italy where he has been hired to paint frescoes on the walls of a church and its tiny baptistery, the building where christenings are held.

Palla Strozzi, an enormously wealthy banker from Florence, commissioned Gentile to paint an altarpiece for the Church of Santa Trinità which would depict the Adoration of the Magi.

When a painter's fame spread, commissions started to come in and this meant he often had to travel by horseback to distant places, accompanied by his assistants who brought his equipment and supplies. Masolino, who came from Panicale, traveled as far as Rome and Hungary for his work, and because he was fascinated by the countryside through which he passed, he recreated it in the background of his paintings. He is now regarded as one of the great pioneers of landscape painting.

The fresco which Masolino has just finished in the baptistery depicts **King Herod's Banquet.**

Masolino discusses his fresco cycle for the Brancacci Chapel in Florence with Filippo Brunelleschi, Donatello and Masaccio. This picture is called The Raising of Tabitha and The Curing of the Lame Man. *To tell these two stories Masolino had to repeat the figure of St. Peter within this unified scene, a device which twenty-five years later was considered old-fashioned. Painters then preferred to show one event at a time.*

Two different colors are used in this schematic drawing to indicate which parts were painted by Masolino (the yellow) and which by Masaccio (the blue) in the fresco on the opposite page.

A true pioneer of Renaissance painting, Masaccio created unforgettable characters in St. Peter Heals the Sick. The figures seem to come right out of the wall toward us, quite a contrast to Masolino's elegant but flat images.

Meanwhile, back in Florence, there was constant discussion and argument among Masolino's fellow painters about volume, space and perspective. Two great artists were at the center of these debates, the architect Filippo Brunelleschi, who was building the dome of Florence Cathedral, and the famous sculptor Donatello. Although Florence was now a city of many differing artistic opinions and trends, Masolino, like Gentile, remained a traditionalist, preferring the world of legend, with its soft colors and glowing light.

When Masolino was asked to paint the frescoes in the Church of Santa Maria del Carmine in Florence, he hired an assistant to help him, a young painter from the same region of Italy he himself came from. Although the assistant's name was Tomaso, he was better known as Masaccio.

It was said that Masaccio, whose father had died and left his family poverty-stricken, arrived in Florence looking for work when he was about twenty. Masolino took him on as a pupil, then later as a partner. From the very beginning, Masaccio had such a different style from his teacher that it is relatively easy to detect who painted what in the paintings they worked on together. Masaccio's style is solid and realistic, his figures conveying a feeling of a real physical presence with the space in which they move reflecting their shape and size.

In his paintings, Masaccio preferred the simple clothes of ordinary people to rich costumes. His faces were highly expressive, with the light coming from one direction, molding his figures. When Masaccio died suddenly in Rome in 1428, at the age of twenty-seven, some contemporary writers declared he was poisoned. "We have suffered a great loss," mourned Brunelleschi. No matter how short his life had been, from that time on, no painter would be able to ignore the brilliant innovations which Masaccio had introduced.

In the peaceful life of a convent, painting became an act of peace and contemplation, almost of prayer, and a special devotion was needed to paint there, a commitment to both God and art. Fra Angelico, who was known as the Blessed Angelico, was perfectly suited to such work. In 1437, the powerful Duke of Florence, Cosimo de' Medici, decided that St. Mark's convent in Florence should be completely renovated under the supervision of the architect Michelozzi. Fra Angelico was commissioned to paint the frescoes in the great communal areas, as well as in the forty-five monks' cells. It was an immense undertaking which Fra Angelico carried out with love and patience. The saints' faces radiate light, their surroundings are precisely drawn and the colors are vividly clear. Each picture is like a vision of Paradise.

This fresco by Fra Angelico which depicts the Annunciation (the moment when the angel Gabriel announces to Mary that she is to be the mother of Jesus) is found in a monk's cell in the convent of San Marco. Although Fra Angelico learned from the new artistic ideas of the day, he did not abandon the delicacy and detail of the old tradition of Gentile and Masolino.

Painters and War

Between the 14th and 15th centuries, most of the free city-states in Italy were taken over by powerful families or military leaders. Political units known as *Signorie*, which were similar to counties, were formed which gradually conquered adjoining territories and absorbed neighboring states. Although a few cities such as Siena, Venice and Genoa continued as republics, they too followed a policy of military power, with frequent wars between the city-states and the various *Signorie*.

Before beginning his painting, Battle of San Romano, *Paolo Uccello makes a quick sketch of a soldier impressively girded in armor.*

Being a soldier became a trade like any other, and a soldier of fortune used any excuse to gird himself in shining armor, gather his followers together and set off for a good fight. In the event of victory, the troops were usually allowed to plunder the surrounding territory as a reward. As usual, the people who suffered most from these military skirmishes were those who were not involved—the local inhabitants.

But only one thought was uppermost in the minds of the warlords: to make sure future generations would remember their glorious achievements. And there was no one who could do that better than a painter.

Paolo di Dono, known as Paolo Uccello, was the undisputed master of these military paintings. In 1456, Cosimo de' Medici asked Uccello to create a painting that would recall the Florentine victory over the Sienese at San Romano. Uccello divided the work into three large paintings on wooden panels which were to decorate a room in the Medici Palace.

Rather than portraying a scene of actual war, Uccello seemed to be depicting a joust between noble knights in a carefully laid-out field of combat. As the battle unfolded in a mass of spears and rearing horses, Uccello's imagination soared. Even the color of the horses owed more to fantasy than fact.

With the help of his assistants, Paolo Uccello is about to transfer the basic outline of his picture, drawn on squares of paper, onto a large piece of wood, or panel, before he begins the actual painting.

One of the three panels for the Battle of San Romano *is finished. The painting shows the moment when the Sienese leader Bernardo della Ciarda has been dislodged from his horse and the soldiers of Florence have finally defeated the army of Siena. Paolo Uccello celebrates the event by inviting friends, apprentices, musicians and jugglers to a grand party. The three panels have since become separated, with this one in Florence, another in London and the third in Paris.*

29

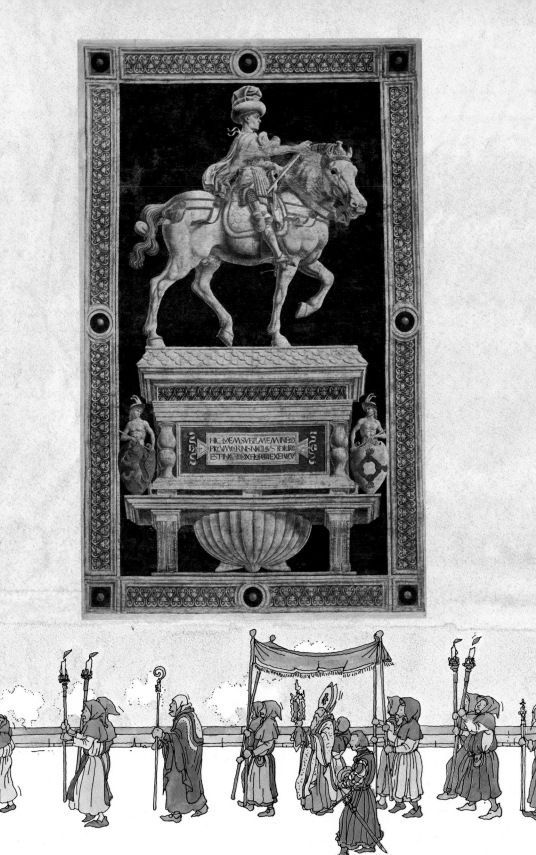

Andrea del Castagno painted the victor of the battle of San Romano, Niccolò da Tolentino, shown here. Although there is only a small range of colors in this huge fresco, the painting is indeed expressive. By the use of clearly drawn lines which emphasize both the taut muscles of the horse and the determined expression of the rider, Andrea was able to convey a remarkable sense of energy and purpose.

Vittore Carpaccio painted St. George and the Dragon, *above, on woven canvas rather than on a wall or on wood. The picture hangs with other Carpaccio paintings in the hall of a scuola, or guild, dedicated to St. George in Venice. If you look carefully you can see the skeletons of all the knights who have tried to kill the dragon.*

Andrea del Castagno's fresco, Portrait of Niccolò da Tolentino, *opposite, can still be seen in Florence Cathedral where it has looked down on religious services for almost 500 years.*

While Florence dominated Tuscany (the region of central Italy that contains Siena and Florence), in the north another Italian city was growing. By the end of the 15th century, Venice had become one of the richest and most important cities in Europe because of its trade. And just as its prosperous merchants and bankers excelled, so its painters, too, began to excel in their craft. This particular canvas is by Vittore Carpaccio, a popular Venetian painter. The knight portrayed here is not a warlord, but a saint, St. George, who killed a dragon in defense of a maiden in distress. Carpaccio included great detail in all his perspective-filled paintings, just as he did in this one.

31

Perspective

The canvas or panel that an artist paints on has only two dimensions—height and width. But an artist also wants to convey space, and space has three dimensions—height, width and depth. The solution to the problem calls for a knowledge of geometrical rules which painters of the past did not possess.

The painter must take into account the position from which a scene is viewed. For instance, if the painter stands on top of a tall building, his view will be broader and the distance to the horizon will be greater than if he were on the ground. He has to decide what size figures in the foreground should be so that they will be in proportion to figures that are at a distance. To get an idea of what is meant by this, hold your thumb up against a window and look at the building behind it. Your thumb appears bigger than the building, but you know the building is bigger, so it must be farther away. The artist must also take into consideration that parallel lines stretching out into the distance (such as the two tracks of a wagon trail) have to come together at a fixed point on the horizon, the so-called vanishing point, in order to give a feeling of distance. When these concepts are applied, a painting has perspective.

Although early painters had no knowledge of these geometrical rules, artists such as Giotto succeeded in surrounding their figures with a feeling of space by an intuitive method that came to be known as pictorial perspective.

One of the earliest painters to be expert at using perspective accurately was Piero della Francesca. Piero was born at Sansepolcro in Central Italy, on the borders of the green rolling countryside of Tuscany and Umbria. He was fond of this Umbrian landscape and used it as a background for his early paintings.

In these black-and-white reproductions of paintings seen earlier, the perspective is wrong, but both have a sense of space. Giotto found it instinctively while Masaccio used a more studied approach. It was only a matter of time before the problem of perspective was solved "scientifically."

The perspective is mathematically perfect in this painting of the Virgin Mary and six saints by Piero della Francesca. It shows Federico di Montefeltro, Duke of Urbino, kneeling in front of the Virgin. The Duke of Urbino paid Piero to paint him in the presence of the Virgin. This is one of the first pictures to show a living person in the same "room" as the Virgin Mary, and the rulers of the Church were unhappy about it. Another unusual feature of the picture is the egg that appears to be hanging over the Virgin's head (if you follow the perspective it is actually some distance behind her). In the 15th century, objects in pictures were often symbols for something. The egg symbolizes eternal life and is placed above the Virgin to show that she will live forever.

33

Unlike many of his fellow artists, Piero della Francesca did not travel much, and in fact, most of his work was done near his birthplace, in the province of Arezzo, and at Urbino. Nevertheless, his paintings had a great influence on his contemporaries, even those living far away.

His most important work was the great series of frescoes depicting the story of the True Cross which can still be seen today in the Church of St. Francis in Arezzo. There is a tradition that St. Helen, the mother of the Roman Emperor Constantine, rediscovered the Cross of Jesus, and the frescoes tell this story.

Piero della Francesca painted this picture of **The Virgin Mary Preparing for Childbirth** *in a small chapel at the cemetery of Monterchi where it can still be seen today. For centuries, pregnant women prayed before it, and even today, before the birth of a child, the local women traditionally bring flowers and light a candle before this beautiful painting.*

Important guests visit Piero della Francesca
as he works in the church of St. Francis at
Arezzo on Hercules' Victory over Cosroe.
When a high wall such as this is to be
painted, special scaffolding is built,
sometimes even equipped with wheels that
can move along the wall, as is seen here.

35

Oil Paints Are Introduced in Flanders

During the early years of the 15th century, Flanders was an exciting place to be. In the rest of Europe, farming was the main occupation, but here in this northern corner of Europe, which is roughly where Belgium and Holland are today, trade and industry were the main activities. Countless towns and villages thrived along Flanders' many canals and rivers.

Flemish artists were doing exciting things too. They were painting with a completely new type of paint that was powder/color mixed with oil. (In Italy paint was made with water and egg yolk.) Although these colors are

A friend visits Jan van Eyck in his studio, probably to admire two of the painter's greatest works, his Madonna with Chancellor Rolin, and his St. Barbara, right.

36

now taken for granted, at that time they were a jealously guarded secret among the Flemish painters. The oil makes the paint dry slowly so that the artist can take his time creating just the shading he wants. Even in very small pictures, the use of the oil paints helped the artists achieve amazingly realistic images.

*The young Jan van Eyck paints
Princess Isabella's portrait in
Lisbon in 1428.*

Jan van Eyck was born toward the end of the 14th century in Flanders, in the province of Limburg. Much of his time was spent working for Philip, the powerful Duke of Burgundy who entrusted Jan with a number of diplomatic missions to the courts of other rulers. The Duke must have been pleased with the results; he raised Jan's pay in 1435 from 100 livres a year to 360 livres, a considerable amount in those days.

Perhaps some of the Duke's satisfaction with Jan came from the completion of a successful mission. Some years earlier, the Duke had become engaged for political reasons to Isabella, the daughter of the King of Portugal. Before marrying his unseen fiancée, the Duke sent Jan, together with other ambassadors, to Portugal to paint the Princess. At the royal court in Lisbon, Jan painted two portraits of Isabella which were sent back to the impatient Duke, one by sea and one by land, in case the other one was lost.

Although neither of the portraits has survived, they must have pleased the Duke, because he and the Princess were married shortly afterward, and Jan himself was among the two thousand people who accompanied Isabella from Portugal to Burgundy for the wedding. Jan van Eyck was, above all, a fine portrait painter with a great eye for detail.

*The Duke of Burgundy is
obviously impressed by the
portrait.*

Rogier van der Weyden's studio in Brussels (where he was the City Painter) is filled with his paintings. On the left is the Adoration of the Magi, *with the Three Wise Men paying homage to the Infant Jesus. At the top is his* Portrait of Antoine de Bourgogne, *a French nobleman, and on the right are the main panel and right wing of a triptych, which is a set of three paintings on hinged panels. This particular triptych, the* Deposition, *shows Jesus being taken down from the cross.*

Rogier van der Weyden, a contemporary and friend of Jan's, was another great Flemish painter. Although there is very little information about him, it is known that he came from an established family of goldsmiths and was a skilled goldsmith himself. He was probably a year or two younger than Jan van Eyck, and he too worked for a long time for the Duke of Burgundy. However, he never signed any of his splendid paintings.

The mathematical perspective that Italian painters found so satisfying did not interest the painters of Flanders. They spent enormous time painting minute detail—the buildings, the animals and the costumes, something they were able to do with their oil-based paints. But it is as if the figures are actors on a stage and the scene in the distance is a painted backdrop. Yet the figures do not lose any power because of a lack of perspective; they may have even more of an impact.

Were oil paints something completely new that the Flemish painters invented? The answer is both yes and no. Actually, painters of ancient Greece, Rome and Byzantium used vegetable oils to dilute their paints, and medieval portrait painters were also aware of the process. However, over the years the complicated method of mixing the paints was lost, at least in the West. So even if the Flemish painters were not the first to use oils, they were probably the first to rediscover the secret.

There are different versions of this rediscovery. One of them tells how Antonello da Messina, a young Sicilian assistant to a Flemish painter, fled to Italy when his master died, taking the secret formula for oil paints with him. The enraged painters of Flanders did everything they could to stop him, including hiring a professional killer. Whether the story is true or not, it is known that the great Sicilian artist, Antonello da Messina, was among the first painters in Italy to use oil paints.

Antonello da Messina shows his colleagues Portrait of a Man, *a beautiful small work that he has done using oil paints.*

Florence and the Medici

In the years after Masaccio's death, the city of Florence, which had grown richer than ever, was controlled by the Medici, a wealthy family of merchants and bankers. The Medici were great patrons of the arts, and launched an incredible period of creativity, perhaps never to be equaled in the history of art. Filippo Brunelleschi had recently completed the vast dome of Florence's cathedral which dominated the whole city. The painters of Florence were busier than ever as the Medici commissioned new palaces and villas and summoned poets, philosophers and artists to their court.

Cosimo de' Medici, a commercial and financial genius, founded the family's immense fortune. The Medici bank had representatives in all the important cities of Europe and it also acted as banker, often with exclusive rights, to the papacy in Rome, the richest state of its time.

Cosimo's political ambitions were fulfilled by his grandson, Lorenzo, who became, in effect, lord of the city, although Florence continued to be called a republic. Lorenzo, who was an even greater supporter of art and antiquity than his grandfather, surrounded himself with the most famous men of arts and letters of the day and gathered the finest minds of Europe at his court. In the second half of the 15th century, man, not technology or the Bible, became the focus of attention, and people began to study the history and poetry of ancient Greece and Rome, as well as tales of the gods and heroes of Greek mythology.

Raphael's father escorts him to Florence to study in Perugino's workshop. In the distance Brunelleschi's famous dome can be seen atop Florence Cathedral.

In an attempt to revive a lost world of beauty, grace and nobility, a whole new range of subject matter was opened up to painters. It was in Florence that Leonardo da Vinci and Michelangelo conducted their first experiments, although it was Sandro Botticelli who truly reflected the spirit of the Medici court. The young Botticelli, who received his artistic education in this environment, transferred onto canvas the images of pure beauty described by the poets, as well as the unrealistic perfection of the worlds of the gods. In *La Primavera* (Spring) Venus is shown holding court in a flower-strewn meadow beneath the shade of an orange grove. The goddess of love, center, dominates the scene, while Cupid hovers, ready to shoot his arrows of love. On the right, Zephyr, the warm wind of spring, dressed in a flowery gown and scattering flowers, pursues Flora. After their marriage, it is Flora who is transformed into Spring. Left, the three Graces dance, symbols of Poetry, Art and Music, while Mercury, the curer, holds up the symbol of medicine. Love triumphs when passion is tempered by art and science, or in other words, by civilization.

Sandro Botticelli painted this enormous picture, La Primavera (Spring), between 1477 and 1478 for a villa belonging to the Medici family. Venus, as well as standing for love and beauty, was also the goddess of learning. Since the painting was destined for the villa of a young Medici, it is thought that it may have been intended to remind the young Medici of the value of virtue and good education. The young man's tutors were friends of Botticelli's and could have suggested the subject to the artist.

During the time of the Medici, Florence was filled with painters' workshops. Now not only the Church provided work for artists, but newly rich traders and businessmen wanted to acquire fine paintings as well. Perugino was one of the busiest and most popular artists of the day. His real name was Pietro Vannucci, but because he worked for a long time in Perugia, he was called Perugino. Besides his talent as an artist, he gained fame because he was the master of Raphael, one of the greatest painters of all time.

Giovanni Santi, Raphael's father, was a fairly successful painter himself when he took his motherless eleven-year-old son, Raffaello, to study under Perugino. Some two years later, Raffaello, now orphaned by the death of his father, was still in Perugino's workshop learning painting skills. Whether Perugino sensed what a brilliant future his new apprentice had is not known, although some say that he became jealous when he realized how talented Raphael was. Perugino may have been jealous, but many years later, Raphael still spoke of his old master with admiration and affection.

Because the great altarpiece, the Adoration of the Magi, is finished, and the artist, Perugino, has gone outside for a moment to meet his friend, Signor Santi's son Raphael, the apprentices relax and have a little fun.

45

Leonardo da Vinci was another great painter whose father took him to Florence, in his case to study under Verrocchio. Leonardo was seventeen at the time. There is a story that, as a young apprentice, Leonardo painted an angel so perfect in a painting of the Baptism of Christ, by his master, that Verrocchio swore he would give up painting. In fact, the painting remains unfinished!

During his apprenticeship, Leonardo became friendly with two other apprentices, Sandro Botticelli and Perugino, although they were both slightly older. In Verrocchio's workshop, the apprentices worked as a group, so it is difficult to tell who did what part of a painting, although sometime shortly after he was twenty, Leonardo signed his first work, an *Annunciation*.

During his lifetime, Leonardo was talented in many fields. As a true Renaissance man, he was an inventor, artist, sculptor, writer, architect, scientist, engineer and botanist who followed up his studies with practical

Leonardo da Vinci's painting of the Annunciation was done when the artist was only twenty years old. It is clear, even at this age, that Leonardo has painted the angel's wings after studying and sketching a real bird and that the Virgin's draperies have been painted from a real piece of cloth, rather than from the imagination. Leonardo continued to study and sketch nature into his old age.

Leonardo, who is fascinated by the flight of birds, studies them with the intention of building a flying machine. His notes on the subject are known as the "Codex on the Flight of Birds."

experiments, leaving behind copious notes and studies on all sorts of subjects. He also planned fortifications, monuments, military machines, canals and locks, and at one time even worked as a military engineer.

Yet, from all this incredible activity, a surprising fact emerges. Leonardo was a great sculptor, but none of his sculptures have survived. As an architect, none of his buildings have survived, nor as a scientist can any specific invention be attributed to him. Of all his art works, only his paintings have endured, and even many of those have been lost.

Leonardo's The Virgin of the Rocks *was painted in 1483. It depicts the Madonna with St. John, the child Jesus and an angel, and derives its name from the enchanted landscape of rocks in the background.*

When Leonardo was in Milan, he worked on a great statue of Ludovico il Moro on horseback, but he had finished only the horse when he was forced to flee the city. Unfortunately, invading French soldiers used the horse as a target for their muskets.

During a time when Leonardo was at the Milan court of Ludovico il Moro, he painted his most important work in the convent of Santa Maria delle Grazie, the great fresco, *The Last Supper.* It has been said that the Prior of the convent complained that Leonardo would come in, stare at the picture for two hours, make six brush strokes and then leave again. Leonardo explained that he was having difficulty visualizing the face of a man as evil as Judas Iscariot, but if the Prior was in a hurry, he would paint in the Prior's face! Unfortunately, Leonardo couldn't resist experimenting: He painted *The Last Supper* with unsatisfactory paints, and the work quickly began to decay. Despite the fresco's poor condition—it has seen countless restorations—the great beauty of the basic design still shines through.

The time Leonardo spent in Milan was perhaps his most productive period as a painter. Besides *The Last Supper,* while he was there he also created the world-famous *The Virgin of the Rocks,* as well as the drawing *Madonna and Child with St. Anne.*

Leonardo's Mona Lisa, *which hangs in the Louvre* *Museum in Paris, is perhaps the most famous* *painting in the world, but Mona Lisa, which means* *Madame Lisa, herself was not famous. She was the* *wife of a Florentine official. Leonardo, however,* *lavished all his skill in painting her portrait. So* *delicately did he wield his brush that only under* *the microscope is it possible to see brush marks.*

Raphael used Leonardo's formula in his Unknown Woman, *also known as* La Muta. *Her face is seen* *almost from the front and her shoulders are only* *half turned outward. More obviously, the hands of* La Muta *are crossed like* Mona Lisa's. *Only an* *artist as great as Raphael could adopt this formula* *and yet still produce a portrait so lovely and so* *different.*

The fascination of Leonardo's painting lies in the way his figures seem to emerge slowly from their background, an illusion Leonardo achieved by blending his colors gently into one another, and by patiently creating effects of light and shade.

Every contour radiates liveliness and tension, with no harsh lines, the *Mona Lisa* being the best example of this technique.

Leonardo enjoyed a long and eventful life which he spent between Florence, Milan and France. Toward the end of his life, he accepted an invitation from Francis I, the King of France who had married Catherine de' Medici. As Leonardo set off on his long and uncomfortable journey to Paris, he took only one small painting with him from Italy, a painting that must have meant a great deal to him, his portrait of *Mona Lisa.* It is said that when Leonardo lay dying, his *Mona Lisa* was at his bedside.

Mantegna receives the title of Palatine Count from the Marquis Ludovico.

An Extraordinary Room

One Italian city after another ended up being controlled by a single family, just the way the Medicis ruled Florence. These new rulers built palaces and villas as luxurious as small royal residences, and their courts competed for the most famous artists, especially painters.

In 1460, Marquis Ludovico III, a member of the Gonzaga family that controlled Mantua, invited Andrea Mantegna, a young painter from Padua, to come to his court. Andrea, who had already done fine paintings at Padua, Verona and Venice, had studied the classical civilizations of Greece and Rome at Padua University and hence was the ideal man for Gonzaga's sophisticated court. Gonzaga offered Andrea fifteen ducats a year, free lodgings and enough wheat for six people. Although Andrea accepted, he couldn't travel to Mantua until he had finished what he was working on in Padua.

After a series of long letters from Ludovico urging Andrea to come— letters which have survived and are of interest today because they show the court life of 15th-century Mantua—Andrea finally arrived and set to work. For the next forty years, he worked for the Gonzaga family, using his impressive talents to meet their needs. He created frescoes, portraits, banners, dinner services, coats of arms and even chests to hold the belongings of young Gonzaga brides.

Over the years he made a good deal more than the original fifteen ducats he was promised. Various members of the Gonzaga family not only gave him houses, villas and farms, but made him a count as well. The whole family looked after him, making sure that his life was as pleasant as

Mantegna arrives in Mantua to join the court of the Gonzaga family.

Mantegna and his young apprentices work in the Bridal Chamber on part of the fresco, Ludovico Gonzaga with his Wife, Children and Courtiers. During the winter months a roaring fire is needed to dry the paint and plaster.

possible. They were so considerate of him, when Giovanni Francesco Gonzaga was away at war and having difficulty finding enough money to pay his soldiers, he wrote home to his wife to make sure that Andrea had received his wages on time.

Similarly, Andrea gave the Gonzaga family the very best of his art. For many years he worked on the walls of a room that lies like a jewel at the heart of Mantua's Ducal Palace, a room that he promised would be the most extraordinary ever seen. Originally it was called the Painted Chamber, but because it contained the portraits of Ludovico and his wife with their court, it came to be known as the Bridal Chamber.

The fresco completed, Mantegna has captured Ludovico
Gonzaga, his family, the members of his court, and even
his hunting dogs frozen in a moment of time so that it is
almost possible to hear their music, gossip and carefree
laughter.

Because the streets of Venice are actually canals, Giovanni Bellini's great altarpiece, carefully wrapped, leaves his studio for its journey by boat to the Church of San Zaccaria.

Andrea Mantegna's wife, Nicolosia, was the sister of Giovanni Bellini, another great painter. Giovanni Bellini and his brother Gentile both worked as artists in Venice. Politically, Venice was different from other Italian cities in that its most powerful families had managed to achieve a balance so that the city had remained a republic, with a ruler known as a Doge as its head. Because there was no royal patron, Giovanni and his brother worked for the Republic, as well as for Venice's countless guilds and trade associations. These organizations, most of which were very wealthy, had their own churches, and because they competed in making them so beautiful, Venice's many churches were decorated with great works of art which are still guarded jealously today.

Giovanni Bellini, together with his brother Gentile, Carpaccio and Giorgione, are regarded as the men who launched the great age of Venetian painting which is famous for the painters' remarkable use of light and color with oil paints. Later, during the 16th century, artistic geniuses such as Titian and Tintoretto continued the tradition.

Giovanni Bellini's great painting, Madonna and Child with Saints, *has safely arrived from the artist's studio and taken its place above the church's altar among the flickering candles.*

The Most Powerful Prince of All

Although there was much competition between the courts of Italian cities, as far as luxury and splendor were concerned, none of them could compete with the Pope. The Pope, who was seated on St. Peter's throne in Rome, wielded spiritual and political power across all the countries of western Europe. He not only received gifts and offerings from around the Roman Catholic world, but he also ruled his own lands (called the Papal States), imposing taxes just like any other prince. The Vatican treasury was so wealthy that it was possible to renovate the great churches of Rome and the Vatican palaces too.

Toward the end of the 15th century, Pope Julius II, a determined and energetic man who was also a clever politician and a fine soldier, summoned Bramante, the great Italian architect, to Rome to work on the church of St. Peter's, as well as other important buildings. Pope Julius II also sought the best artists and sculptors for his projects, favoring Raphael and Michelangelo, the two 16th-century artistic titans who worked for years painting frescoes on the walls and ceilings of the Vatican's chapels and apartments.

Raphael completed two great frescoes which decorate the Signature Room in the Vatican Palace, and these form part of the magnificent series known as the Vatican Room frescoes. In his own personal style, he combined the experimentation and research that had been developed by numerous Renaissance painters: Piero della Francesca's mastery of

Raphael shows the Pope the sketches he has made for some frescoes.

Before they can begin on such a huge and complicated series of frescoes, Raphael and his assistants have to spend time in study and preparation.

57

perspective; the solemnity and grandeur of Mantegna's landscape
backgrounds; the powerful modeling of Michelangelo's figures; Leonardo
da Vinci's delicate shading techniques; and the Venetians' use of color.
One can only imagine what he would have accomplished had he lived
longer. Tragically for the world, Raphael died in Rome in 1520 at the age of
thirty-six. He had not finished his work on the Vatican Rooms.

Raphael's frescoes decorate the Vatican room. In the fresco on the left, The Dispute over the Sacrament, Raphael has portrayed the learned men of Christianity (below), watched over by Christ and the saints (above) and linked together by the Holy Sacrament (center). The Holy Trinity, Father, Son, and Holy Ghost (in the form of a dove) is directly above the Sacrament. On the lower level, among the Doctors of the Church, are the Italian poet Dante, the reformer Savonarola and Pope Sixtus IV, wearing gold ceremonial robes. In the fresco on the right, known as the School of Athens, symbols for Truth and Faith are joined by Philosophy and Science, which represent human reason. Besides Aristotle and Plato, who are seen in the center, Pythagoras is seen writing on a tablet, left, and Euclid drawing on a slate on the ground, right. Bramante, Leonardo da Vinci, Michelangelo and Raphael himself are also portrayed in this magnificent fresco.

The Start of Printing

In the closing years of the 14th century, Johann Gensfleisch, better known to history as Johann Gutenberg, was born in Mainz, Germany. He was close to forty years old when he developed a system of movable letter-blocks covered in ink that allowed large numbers of copies of any written work to be printed. Until that time, books had been written entirely by hand, but now, thanks to Gutenberg, the printed book was born.

It was natural that Gutenberg's new process would catch on rapidly in Nuremberg, Germany, an important cultural and economic center. Anton Koberger, the first German publisher, opened a workshop there in 1470 with forty printing presses and a hundred employees.

What an incredible impact this invention had, not only for writers, but for painters too. Now pictures, as well as words, could be almost endlessly reproduced. One of the first artists to take advantage of this new process was another German, Albrecht Dürer.

Albrecht Dürer is seated at his writing desk. Dürer's drawings, his watercolors and, above all, his engravings are generally far superior to his oil paintings, but this beautiful oil painting, Feast of the Rose Garlands, is an exception.

In Dürer's day, the text of a book was composed using the new, movable letters invented by Gutenberg, each letter made of a small block of hard wood carved by hand. Once the text for an entire page is accurately assembled, the whole block is inked and pressed onto a damp sheet of paper by means of the great press shown here. The illustrations for the text, such as Dürer's Rhinoceros, seen here, are printed the same way. Each illustration is drawn separately on a small, carefully smoothed block of wood and then patiently carved. The design is later inked and pressed onto damp paper, just like the text.

Dürer, who was born in Nuremberg in 1471, worked as a draftsman in his father's gold- and silversmith workshop. He was only thirteen when he penciled a self-portrait that revealed his considerable talent. His artistic skills included not only his drawings, but the engravings he created for printing purposes as well.

Dürer's skill in engraving the copper and wood plates used for printing was matchless, and the engravings themselves had many benefits. They could easily be carried on horseback, which was difficult or impossible with a large painting. This in turn meant that Dürer's fame spread quickly throughout Europe. And on Dürer's extensive travels, whenever he saw a picture he liked he would have an engraving made, since an engraving provided a better pictorial translation than a drawing and lasted longer.

Dürer traveled all over Germany, to the Low Countries and twice to Italy, studying some of the great Flemish and Italian painters. His art developed a richness of detail that was characteristic of the Flemish masters combined with a sense of inspired grandeur that was typical of the Italian Renaissance.

Dürer has just completed a fine print from his **Little Passion** *series of woodcuts. Damp paper is used because it adheres better to the engraved block, so after the printing process is finished, the pages have to be hung up to dry.*

Germany, Land of Painters

During the 16th century, Germany saw the rise of a whole generation of great painters, particularly in the south where the patronage of local princes and bishops led to a real flowering of the arts. This period is sometimes known as the German Renaissance.

Although a good deal is known about Albrecht Dürer, almost nothing is known about another fine painter, Grünewald. Actually, Grünewald was ignored for centuries and his works attributed to other painters, such as Dürer and Cranach, which is strange, considering that Grünewald's imagination and the strong emotional content of his paintings clearly distinguish his style from his contemporaries.

The highly imaginative and visionary Grünewald is attracted to subjects filled with mystical experience and temptation, such as St. Anthony who is seen here in St. Anthony and St. Paul *and* Temptation of St. Anthony. *When these panels are opened, they reveal in the center a group of carvings that are normally hidden.*

Altdorfer, the artist who "invented" landscape painting, allows the setting and landscape to play a more important role than the figures, as is evident here in Susannah.

Possibly Grünewald's greatest work was the *Isenheim Altarpiece* which he painted for St. Anthony's convent at Isenheim in Alsace. The altarpiece is a huge polyptych made up of six panels, two fixed and four movable. The four movable panels were painted on both sides so that when they were open—like the pages of a huge book—the altar presented three different faces.

Albrecht Altdorfer, another great artist of the German Renaissance, arrived in Regensburg with his painter father, Ulrich, in 1505 and lived there until his death in 1538. An engraver and architect, as well as a painter, Altdorfer was responsible for designing the city's fortifications and many of its buildings. Although Altdorfer's paintings reflect his skill at architectural drawing, his main contribution to art was his introduction of landscape as a subject in its own right and not just as a background. Altdorfer, like Grünewald, was a court painter and enjoyed the patronage of men such as Duke Wilhelm IV of Bavaria, who commissioned a great series of historical paintings from a number of different artists.

Lucas Cranach, whose name was derived from his birthplace, was born in 1472 in the town of Kronach in Franconia. Although he spent his early years working in his father's studio, he was invited as a young man to the court of the Electors of Saxony in Wittenberg where he became an important figure in the city, at one point even serving as its mayor. Except for a short but important stay in Vienna when he was young, Cranach spent his life in Wittenberg, dying there in 1553.

Cranach's epitaph described him as *pictor celerrimus* (a very speedy painter), and indeed he did hundreds of paintings that now hang in countless museums and private collections. He ran a well-organized studio, employing many assistants, among whom were his sons, Hans and Lucas, the latter being known as Cranach the Younger to distinguish him from his father.

Venus and Cupid *is one of Cranach's many paintings with a mythological theme.*

Cranach spent some time in Vienna where he painted the Crucifixion. His paintings from this period have a much more personal feeling than the ones he painted later, which seem almost mass produced. In Cranach's works, drama and emotion are always tempered by a precise and elegant sense of line.

Cranach's vast artistic output included many portraits of Martin Luther and other important Protestant leaders which he painted in order to spread Protestantism. He also painted many female nudes from mythology, including Venus and the Three Graces. These elegant but rather cold women reflected the ideals of female beauty which prevailed in the German courts of Cranach's day.

The great period of German painting ended with Hans Holbein, called the Younger to distinguish him from his father who was a well-known Augsburg painter. Three countries—Germany, England and Switzerland—all compete for the honor of being Holbein's homeland. Actually, Holbein was an international artist. He spent his childhood in Augsburg, Germany, where he was trained in his father's studio, learning much from his father's circle of artists. He then moved on to Switzerland, and in Basle received many important commissions, such as the fresco decorations for the Council Chamber.

While he was in Basle he married, then moved on again in 1532, this time to England where he became court painter to King Henry VIII with an annual salary of £30, less £3 tax. He died of the plague in London in 1543, at the age of forty-six, still in the prime of his artistic life.

Holbein enjoyed his life at King Henry's court and spoke of England with great warmth. One of his tasks as court painter was to paint portraits of the King's prospective brides. That turned out to be quite a long-standing job, considering that Henry, who rejected the Pope's authority and introduced divorce, had six wives.

For Henry's second wife, Anne Boleyn, Holbein created a triumphal arch to mark her entry into London. A few years later, after Anne had been put to death, Holbein painted Henry's portrait with Jane Seymour, his third wife. Jane Seymour produced the male heir that Henry had longed for, but

Although Holbein is working on a portrait of Henry VIII, the king is too busy with affairs of state to pose. A straw model, dressed in the clothes that the king wore for his marriage to Anne of Cleves, is sitting in for him. On the wall is Holbein's portrait of Sir Thomas More, one of Henry's ministers who was later condemned to death for his opposition to the Reformation. Next to it is the picture of Sir Thomas's whole family that Holbein painted during his first stay in England.

Henry VIII seems pleased with Holbein's finished portrait of him.

she died only a year after their marriage, and Holbein was sent to various European cities to paint portraits of possible new wives for the king. In Brussels he painted Christine of Denmark, in Le Havre, it was Louise of Guise, in Nancy, it was Anne of Lorraine, in Joinville, Renata of Guise, and finally, in Düren, he painted Amalia and Anne of Cleves. Although Anne of Cleves became Henry's fourth wife, he divorced her too, and the process of finding a new wife started all over again.

Holbein is considered one of the greatest portrait painters of all time, and it is thanks to him that likenesses of such great men as Sir Thomas More and Erasmus, as well as a fine self-portrait drawing, exist today. Holbein worked objectively, painting an exact facial likeness of his subjects, along with hints of their social standing. A detached portraitist, he presented his subjects without drama, and without expressing either approval or disapproval.

69

A Painter with Stone Fever

Luckily, Lodovico Buonarroti entrusted his new son, Michelangelo, to a nurse whose whole family worked as stone masons. At an early age, Michelangelo caught "stone fever," as he himself called it, and he was started on the road to becoming a sculptor. Being a strong-willed person as well, Michelangelo refused to settle into a comfortable and respected career as a public official as his father wanted him to. Throughout his long life (he lived to be ninety) Michelangelo considered himself to be a sculptor, as well as an architect. His many statues, both finished and unfinished, and his marvelous dome for St. Peter's in Rome, which was his greatest architectural achievement, certainly justify this view.

Nevertheless, Michelangelo is best remembered for a painting. Pope Clement VII asked him to cover the altar wall of the Sistine Chapel in the Vatican with frescoes, the greatest feat of painting ever undertaken. Several years earlier, Michelangelo had painted a series of breathtaking figures on the Chapel ceiling; and now he was being asked to tackle the altar wall which was almost fourteen meters high and thirteen meters wide.

In his shop, Michelangelo works on marble sculptures for the Medici tombs, copying sketches he made that rest on his easel.

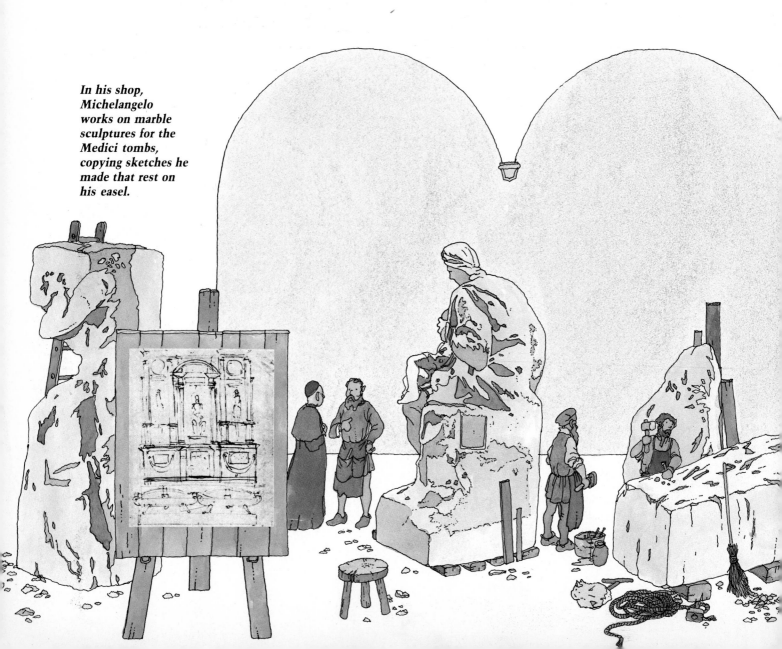

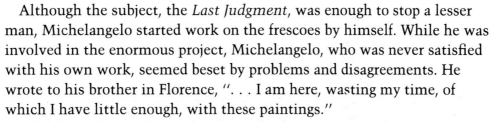

Although the subject, the *Last Judgment*, was enough to stop a lesser man, Michelangelo started work on the frescoes by himself. While he was involved in the enormous project, Michelangelo, who was never satisfied with his own work, seemed beset by problems and disagreements. He wrote to his brother in Florence, ". . . I am here, wasting my time, of which I have little enough, with these paintings."

Michelangelo may have considered the fresco a waste of time, but his interest in the human body—which provided the subject of all his works—reached triumphant heights in the tangled mass of limbs in the *Last Judgment*. The fresco depicts the moment at the end of the world when Jesus Christ judges each person to have been good or evil and whether he or she should go to heaven or hell. Undoubtedly, this fresco on the altar wall of the Sistine Chapel is one of the world's greatest paintings. Many churches had pictures of the *Last Judgment* above the altar to remind the congregation that only by attending church could they be saved from going to hell.

Before the sculptures for the tombs are finished, Michelangelo moves to Rome. He is there only a few days before Pope Clement VII, who had commissioned him to paint The Last Judgment, *dies. The new pope, Paul III, not only asks Michelangelo to continue the painting, but he also gives Michelangelo the official title of Painter, Sculptor, and Architect of the Vatican Palace.*

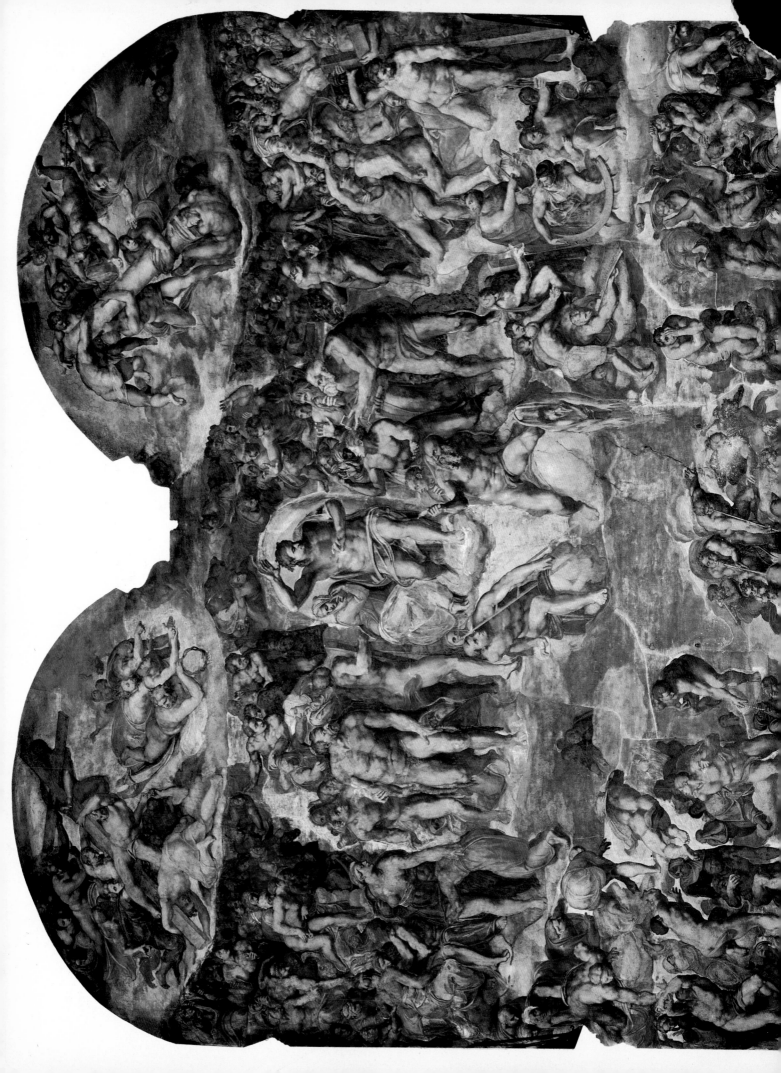

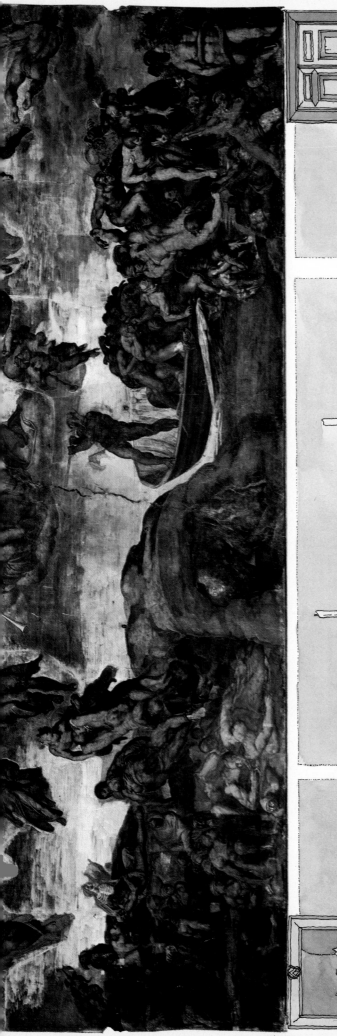

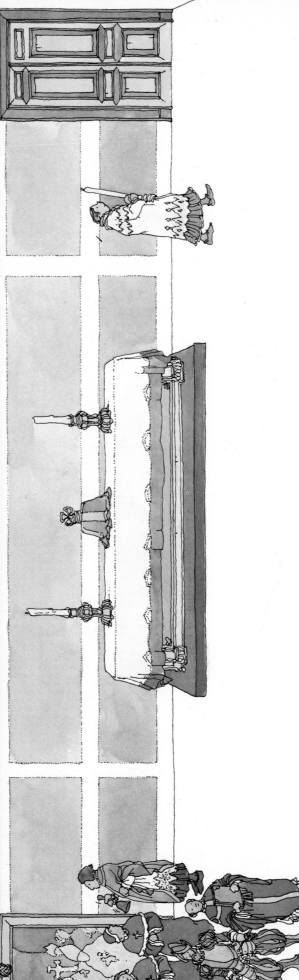

Michelangelo originally painted all the figures in The Last Judgment naked. Some years later, the members of the Vatican hierarchy decided that nudity in a church was shocking, and they asked the painter Daniele da Volterra to clothe them in trousers. From that time on, Daniele became known as "Il Brachettone," the trouser-maker.

73

The Great Years of Venice

During the time that the popes were making Rome the artistic capital of
Italy, Venice was locked in conflict with a terrifying enemy, the Turks.
The Turks not only seized Byzantium, the ancient city of Constantinople,
and made it their capital, but they also gave it the name it still bears today:

Giorgione's beautiful painting The Castelfranco
Madonna *hangs in the Church of San Liberale in
Giorgione's hometown of Castelfranco Veneto. Although
it was thought for a long time that the soldier with the
lance was St. George, it is actually a portrait of the
military leader who commissioned the painting, Tuzio
Costanzo.*

Istanbul. Although the Turks were destroying Venice's trade by overrunning her possessions in the Middle East, Venetian painting, led by the three greatest names of the day—Giorgione, Titian and Tintoretto—was in its most glorious period.

The story of Giorgione is a strange one. He had enormous success, and was so famous during his own lifetime that his works became legendary, but today almost nothing is known about him. In fact, two or three hundred years after his death, the art historians who were trying to separate the legends from the truth began to doubt that he had ever really existed! Now it is known that he was born at Castelfranco Veneto, probably around 1477, and that he was one of the great painters of his day.

In contrast to Giorgione, all sorts of facts are known about Titian, who was born in 1490 in Pieve di Cadore; every step of his long life can be traced by the letters and documents he left behind. Titian had successes, but he also had terrible arguments about money with his patrons, the rulers of the time, including the Pope, as well as Emperor Charles V, who considered Titian his favorite painter.

During his stay in Rome in 1546, Titian painted this portrait, Pope Paul III with His Grandsons. Alessandro, a cardinal, and Ottavio, a famous soldier, as well as the Pope, are members of the powerful and noble Farnese family. Titian was the greatest portrait painter of his day. The change from intimate bust-sized portraits to the huge life-size portraits of the mid-16th century is credited to Titian.

Giorgione and Titian had been born within the territory of the Venetian Republic, but Jacopo Robusti, who was known as Tintoretto, was born in the very heart of Venice in the San Cassiano district in 1518, at a time when Titian's career had just taken off. His father, Giovan Battista Robusti, was a dyer (*tintore*) by trade and Jacopo's nickname, Tintoretto, means "little dyer."

Although the Turks had recently occupied Constantinople, the Venetians themselves had conquered the city during the Crusades, a victory which had marked the beginning of their rise to power. Perhaps to give heart to the citizens of Venice, who were concerned by the advance of the Turkish Empire, the Venetian State commissioned Tintoretto to create a series of paintings that would recall the great victory of their ancestors.

There is a story that Tintoretto studied in Titian's workshop but that Titian threw him out after only ten days. It is certainly true that their artistic styles were very different. Titian's solemnity was in direct opposition to the younger Tintoretto's restless and exuberant temperament. In his lifetime, Titian became a painter for the great courts of Europe, while Tintoretto was destined to spend his life adorning the churches and confraternities of his native Venice.

This painting by Tintoretto, Battle Between Pirates, *is based on an actual sea battle between the Venetians and the Turks. Tintoretto has added a scene from mythology, the abduction of Helen.*

Two Great Solitary Figures

At last Venice managed to convince the other European powers that the Turks were a threat, and in 1571 they formed an alliance which defeated the Turkish Sultan's fleet at Lepanto. Although the Venetians did not regain their former dominance of the seas, the Turkish advance was halted, and the victory was celebrated throughout Europe as a great triumph for Christianity.

This work by El Greco has been called at various times The Dream of Philip II, The Universal Judgment, or The Adoration of the Name of Jesus. Interpreted as an allegory, the painting shows the European rulers who formed the Holy League, which defeated the Turks at Lepanto, surrounding the central figure of Pope Pius V. To the right of Pius is Don John of Austria, the admiral of the victorious Christian fleet at Lepanto. The two figures kneeling in thanks to the Pope and Don John are Philip II of Spain, in black, and next to him, the Venetian Doge, Alvise Mocenigo.

The Turkish-held island of Crete was not far from   , and it was
     here, some thirty years before the Battle of Lepant   that Domenikos
Theotokopoulos, the artist known as El Greco, the Greek, was born. When
the battle took place, El Greco was in Venice where he achieved his early
fame as a follower of Titian. An historian of that day recounts that there
was a Greek painter living in Italy who painted magnificent works in the
manner of Titian, but who suddenly changed his style and painted ugly,
strange figures.

Apparently, El Greco had become very full of himself; in fact it was his
arrogance that eventually caused him to flee Italy. When Pope Pius V
proposed having the nudes in Michelangelo's *Last Judgment* covered, El
Greco is supposed to have suggested that the whole fresco be demolished
and that he would paint another as good and pleasant to look at.
Presumably, this caused such a furor that El Greco moved to Spain, where
he remained until his death.

Although his highly individual style did not find much favor with his
contemporaries, today El Greco is regarded as one of the greatest and most
original artists of his time.

*El Greco, who lived in Spain for
forty years, paints the* Pentecost,
*one of his many mystical religious
works which give full rein to his
visionary style. The painting
depicts the Virgin Mary and the
Apostles gathering after the death
of Jesus to receive the Holy Spirit
on the day known as Pentecost.*

Another great artist of the 16th century was Pieter Bruegel, called the Elder to distinguish him from his son, who was also a painter. Very little is known of Bruegel's life, and two small villages near Breda, one in Holland and one in Belgium, both vie for the honor of being his birthplace.

Bruegel's paintings are unique, far removed from the mainstream of European art championed by artists such as Titian and Tintoretto. He was not interested in the great events of the day, the courts of Europe, or important historical characters. Instead, he turned his attention to the peasants, leaving a fascinating record of their everyday life during the 16th century.

Many different scenes are portrayed within Pieter Bruegel's **Flemish Proverbs***, each of which illustrates a popular saying. In the middle at the front a man fills in a hole after the calf has drowned; he gives advice when it is too late. To the left, one man shears a pig, another a sheep; one has all the profit, the other has nothing. At the top of the picture are scenes of two more proverbs: a man trails his cloak in the wind; another throws feathers to the wind.*

Light and Shade

Toward the end of the 16th century, a new problem began to attract the attention of painters: how to paint light. Figures and objects change as the light around them changes. A diffuse light emphasizes color, but tends to flatten out objects, while a bright light creates special patterns of shadows that draw attention to shape and volume.

Michelangelo Merisi, known as Caravaggio, was a pioneer in this field, and the contrast between light and shade (called chiaroscuro) lies at the heart of his painting. His figures emerge from the dense shadows that surround them as though they were floodlit. Frozen at a precise moment in time, they convey a feeling of strength and drama.

Michelangelo Merisi was born in 1573 in the town of Caravaggio from which he derived his name. He began his career in nearby Milan, then moved to Rome where he created his most important pictures. Opinion was strongly divided over his work, with some praising it and others sneering at it. Perhaps it was these mixed reactions that led to his emotional problems.

Caravaggio spent many years in a tangle of brawls, duels, accusations and pardons. Finally he killed a man, was wounded himself, and was forced to flee, first to Naples and then to Malta. As his artistic fame grew, and his original style began to capture the imagination of his contemporaries, Caravaggio did everything he could do to obtain a pardon from the Pope. When the pardon was finally granted, it was too late. He died of a fever at the age of thirty-seven, alone and in despair.

The Conversion of St. Paul, *left, hanging in Caravaggio's studio, depicts St. Paul falling from his horse on the road to Damascus in response to a great light in the sky. Although portrayed realistically, Caravaggio makes the scene look more like an accident in a stable than one of the Bible stories. In* The Martyrdom of St. Peter, *right, Caravaggio concentrates more on the effort needed to raise the cross into position than he does on the saint's upside-down crucifixion. Because he often represented holy figures with peasant faces and showed life as it really was, Caravaggio shocked a number of his contemporaries.*

Caravaggio fled from Naples to Malta where he is seen opposite painting portraits of some of the Knights of Malta. Unfortunately, he insulted an important dignitary and was forced to flee Malta as well.

In Germany, another great painter, Peter Paul Rubens, was also experimenting with light. Where Caravaggio used light to create darkly dramatic figures that seem to have been dragged out of the gloom by a lantern, Rubens filled his canvases with a warm, radiant glow that conveyed joy and life. In contrast to Caravaggio, Rubens, who achieved fame and prosperity as a painter, also enjoyed a full and happy personal life.

Rubens was born in Germany (actually, at Siegen in Westphalia) where his father had been exiled, although when he was young, his family returned to Antwerp, a city that he always considered home. In 1600 Rubens traveled to Italy where he was attracted by the reputation of Italian painting and where he worked for almost ten years. He stayed in Venice, Mantua and finally Rome. There he was deeply impressed by Caravaggio's paintings. When he finally returned to Antwerp, he discovered that his fame as a painter had preceded him.

Below, Rubens' triptych shows The Descent from the Cross, *center, with* The Visitation, *left, and* The Presentation in the Temple, *right. Interestingly, the clothes are the dress of the early 17th century.*

With commissions and requests coming from all over Europe, Rubens was able to build himself a beautiful townhouse in the Italian style. He had so many pupils working in his immense studio that he ultimately had a gallery built where spectators could view his work-in-progress just as if they were in a theater.

Rubens greatly influenced contemporary tastes, and although his hands were crippled with arthritis and gout, he worked hard until the end of his life. When he died in 1640, all of Europe mourned his passing.

Rubens hosts a reception in his luxurious home in Antwerp. In his paintings he carefully reproduces the extravagant costumes of the day.

Rubens' painting of Marie de' Medici's wedding is part of a series of paintings depicting her life. Marie, who was a descendant of Lorenzo the Magnificent, married King Henry IV of France, although the man facing her here in *The Marriage by Proxy in Florence is not the King, but an official standing in for him. The wedding took place in Florence, while the King was in France.*

Rembrandt van Rijn was born in 1606 in the Dutch city of Leyden where he attended the Latin school and later Leyden University. Although his parents hoped he would become a clergyman or a magistrate, Rembrandt showed such a talent for drawing that his father, a wealthy miller, took him out of school and placed him in the city's school of painting.

Toward the end of the 16th century, Holland, after decades of struggle, finally gained its freedom from Spain and declared itself a republic, thereby separating from the southern Low Countries (modern Belgium). The new Dutch state, which became a major sea power with a flourishing worldwide trade, produced a rich and powerful class of merchants and shop owners who, like the Flemish, were also interested in painting. It was a remarkable period of economic and artistic development.

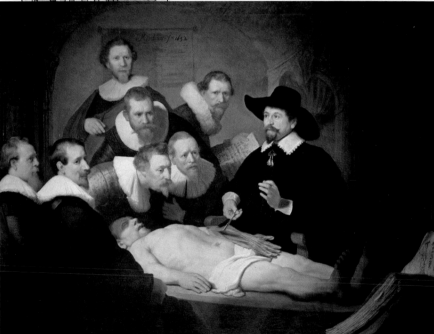

In **The Anatomy Lesson of Dr. Tulp,** *Rembrandt has painted Dr. Tulp demonstrating the anatomy of a hand and explaining its function. The corpse the surgeon is dissecting so realistically is that of a man who was hanged for robbery.*

*During the 17th century, Old Amsterdam,
clustered around the mouth of the Amstel River,
was extended by the construction of three
concentric canals. With handsome homes of
prosperous Dutch merchants springing up around
the canals, Old Amsterdam is a famous example of
early town-planning.*

Within a few decades, Amsterdam became a major capital of Europe and
Rembrandt opened his studio there, introducing himself to the public with
a spectacular painting, *The Anatomy Lesson of Dr. Tulp*, Dr. Tulp being
the chief surgeon in Amsterdam. Rembrandt's genius was immediately
recognized and the city leaders clamored to have him paint their portraits.
Everything seemed to be going well for Rembrandt. He became rich,
enjoyed a brilliant social life in Amsterdam and married Saskia, a beautiful
girl who became his favorite model.

Various companies of ex-soldiers wanted to commemorate Holland's victory over the Spanish, and Rembrandt was commissioned to paint a huge canvas portraying *The Company of Captain Frans Banning Cocq*. The more familiar title of the painting is *The Night Watch*, a title it acquired over the centuries as neglect and accumulated dirt darkened its tones. Since it has been cleaned, it is obvious that the scene takes place in daylight.

It seems strange that a masterpiece by such a genius as Rembrandt could remain unnoticed for so long. But public tastes change, and *The Night Watch* because of its extremes of darkness and light produced varied public reactions at the time, and signaled the beginning of Rembrandt's decline. Nevertheless, as a serious painter, Rembrandt continued to develop and express his own personal style, refusing to cater to public opinion in order to gain success. Forced to declare bankruptcy, in 1669, alone, bitter, and abandoned by his friends, Rembrandt died.

Rembrandt's The Night Watch *is displayed with other portraits of military companies in the great hall of the Civil Guard in Amsterdam. This is far from a traditional portrait in which the soldiers appear in neat, military order; it is rather a visual record of the actual historical moment when the captain gives the order for a company at arms to march off. In comparison, it makes other military paintings of the day look as stiff as scenes on a playing card. Interestingly enough, each man in the company had to pay for his share of the cost of the painting, 160 florins in all.*

Royal Portraits

Portrait painting, which was well-established in Italy, spread throughout the courts of Europe during the 16th century, achieving new heights of popularity in the 17th century. It was a period when the great European monarchies consolidated, and a new and powerful middle class emerged. Portraits now provided a record of the lives of the ruling houses or the great financial and commercial families. Rather than a record of a specific historical event or military victory, portraits now became a means of displaying their subject's power and prestige.

Anthony van Dyck, who was a great Flemish artist and contemporary of Rubens and

Portrait of Cardinal Guido Bentivoglio, *which van Dyck is painting here in Italy, reveals strong echoes of Titian, a painter whom van Dyck greatly admired, although the portrait's minute attention to detail is in the Flemish tradition.*

In the subject's pose and in the range of colors he uses, van Dyck's portrait of his patron, King Charles I, has a feeling of Rubens' paintings, although van Dyck's style is more restrained.

Rembrandt, lived in northern Europe at this time. He had trained under Rubens in Antwerp and remained there until 1620 when, at twenty, he was summoned to work at the court of James I in England. In 1632 he returned to England (during the reign of Charles I), settling outside London, where the King used to visit him. Soon after his return, van Dyck was given an apartment in Eltham Castle in Kent which you can see above. More than five hundred portraits by van Dyck have survived, many of which were painted in Italy, particularly in Genoa, which was his base during his stay there.

Velazquez is working on Las Meninas, *with the Infanta Margarita posed in the center, surrounded by her court ladies. Behind them is Velazquez's equestrian portrait,* Philip IV of Spain.

During the same period, Diego Velazquez was painting portraits in Madrid. His career in the formal and strict court of the Spanish Hapsburgs was proceeding slowly, until in 1646, at the age of forty-seven, he was appointed to the post of valet de chambre to the King. It was not until 1658 that he became a Knight of St. James, an honor he had long hoped for. Two years later when he died, he was buried with all the honors that were due to one of his rank.

Because there were strict rules in Spain which governed how official portraits could be painted, Velazquez's most interesting works were nonofficial: portraits of jesters, dwarfs and maids. These colorful characters existed in the shadow of the Royal Court, and Velazquez was free to paint them as he pleased, without any restrictions.

Velazquez was a court painter, so he had few opportunities to paint religious pictures, and mythologies were rare in Spain. Therefore when on a visit to the Spanish court, Rubens suggested that Velazquez go to Italy, Velazquez took him up on the idea. For two years he painted biblical and mythological subjects and many nudes.

Velazquez, who was fond of painting royalty, did this portrait, Philip IV of Spain, when the king was a young man. Velazquez was a slow worker, with a steady technique; there are no flamboyant brush strokes in his paintings. His backgrounds tended to make his portrait figures stand out rather than blend in with them.

95

Although there were no kings or cardinals in the mostly Protestant 17th-century Dutch republic, individuals who had achieved a place in high society because of their prestige or money (or both) often commissioned portraits of themselves. The trade and craft associations known as guilds frequently commissioned commemorative portraits of their governors or members, as did certain military companies. Aside from Rembrandt, Frans Hals was the most able painter of such subjects.

Frans Hals, a man with no intellectual or moral pretentions, is an instinctive and spontaneous painter interested in real, contemporary life. His Portrait of W. van Heythusen is remarkable because of the sitter's unusual pose.

Hals painted portraits of the men of the time, catching their likenesses with bold brushstrokes which were characteristic of his style. Although Hals's approach to perspective was rather simplistic, and his paintings lacked scenery, their vitality and spontaneity brought his figures to life.

Hals, who was not particularly well regarded as an artist in his lifetime, led what could only be described as a disorganized life. Partly as a result of having countless children from two marriages, Hals was almost always short of money, and during one particularly bad winter, the city council of Haarlem, where he lived, had to send him three loads of turf so that he could heat his home.

The Last Glimmers of the 17th Century

During the second half of the 17th century, Dutch control of the seas weakened as England's position became increasingly stronger. Following the marvelous era of Rembrandt, the Dutch became more inward-looking, a trend that extended to their painting as well. Once again, artists began to concern themselves with the portrayal of simple, intimate interiors.

The Dutch painter Vermeer, who was a generation younger than Rembrandt, became a master of this new era. His greatness, however, did not lie in his subjects, which were scenes from everyday life, but in the

*Vermeer, seen here in his studio, is painting a model posing as Fame for his **Allegory of Painting (The Painter in His Studio)** which he created for the society of painters in his hometown of Delft. On the left are three of his best-known works, all featuring the windows which are so important to his work: **The Milkmaid** (top left), **The Love Letter** (top right) and **Girl Reading by a Window** (bottom).*

way he conveyed a mood of gentle intimacy. By the use of light and color, he was able to paint silence and solitude. A dense and almost tangible early morning light filters through a window, flooding the room, and enveloping everything in it, even penetrating the folds of material. Like a thin, semi-transparent veil, color shimmers with infinite variations of light and shade.

It seems almost unbelievable that a genius such as Vermeer remained unknown until the 19th century, but it was not until Etienne Thoré, a French revolutionary who fought in the 1848 Revolution, devoted his time in exile to studying art, in particular Vermeer, that Vermeer's works were "rediscovered."

A single theme appears again and again in the works of certain painters. In Vermeer, it was the interior of a house with light streaming through a window to the left, while in Georges de la Tour's canvases it was a candlelight scene. This repetition often produced uninspired, stereotyped works in artists of limited talent. Although la Tour occasionally fell into this trap, his great skills as a painter prevented his use of candlelight from becoming merely a means of creating a theatrical effect.

Despite the advances made by Caravaggio in the portrayal of light and shade, painters in Italy and elsewhere continued to work in the traditions of the past throughout the 17th century. These traditional painters, called Mannerists, regarded Michelangelo, Raphael and the great 16th-century Venetian masters as their absolute sources of inspiration and style. Two brothers, Annibale and Agostino Carracci, and their cousin Ludovico, were Mannerists who worked in Bologna and Rome at the end of the 16th century and the beginning of the 17th.

In a Mannerist painting, the figure is generally the main feature, often in a distorted pose and with emphasized muscles. The subject is never taken from life, but usually from mythology, and there is often no relationship in scale between the figures in the background and the figures in the foreground.

Like most 17th-century European painters, Georges de la Tour was influenced to some extent by Caravaggio, as can be seen here in Virgin with Child, *in which the strong contrast between light and shade creates a mood of pathos and dreamy intimacy.*

Annibale Carracci, who has been brought to Rome by
Cardinal Farnese in 1595, is seen here working on
Polyphemus Attacking Acis and Galatea, a detail of the
fresco which will adorn the great ceiling of the Gallery in
the Farnese Palace.

The Roman Catholic Church responded to the Protestant Reformation with its own Counter-Reformation, reaffirming traditional principles and dogmas of faith throughout the Catholic world. Although Baroque painters reinforce this Counter-Reformation in their art, Murillo's religious paintings, such as Madonna and Child, *shown here, consistently reflect basic human emotions and the deep spiritual feelings of ordinary people.*

As England's control of the seas strengthened, the Spanish Empire began to weaken. Even when Spain was at its most prosperous, the common people lived a miserable existence, but with Spain's decline, their living conditions became almost intolerable. The streets of Spanish cities were filled with beggars and children dressed in rags. It was from this poverty-stricken world that Bartolomé Esteban Murillo painted his subjects, often portraying the street children of his home town of Seville. The 17th century, which was a troubled period of wars, plagues and famines, provided many other painters with realistic subject matter.

When the churches and convents of Seville commissioned Murillo to create altarpieces and devotional paintings, Murillo drew inspiration from the common people, using them as models for his religious figures and showing everyday life without trying to glorify it. He expressed his simple and straightforward religious feelings in delicate and tender images.

England During the 18th Century

The 18th century marked a period of revival and relative prosperity in Europe. With her great colonial empire, her powerful trading position and her increasing industrialization, England was best able to enjoy the rewards of this new prosperity.

English high society, which had grown rich from commercial ventures, began to build luxurious houses somewhat in the manner of Italian 16th-century palaces. Because people sought paintings to decorate their fine homes, painting flourished in England. The Royal Academy was founded in 1768, with King George III as its patron, and Sir Joshua Reynolds, a painter, as its first president. For the first time, exhibitions of contemporary paintings were shown in London, inciting interest and ensuring the success of England's most talented artists.

Reynolds, whose *Discourses* on painting became the guide for young English artists, dominated the scene, traveling widely in Italy and Flanders. Because he also knew the major literary figures of the day, he was his country's most cultured artist and the one most suited to provide the impetus behind England's artistic flowering.

Although Reynolds was a brilliant portrait painter, he also painted historical subjects, which at that time were considered to be the highest form of art. His most prestigious commission, *The Family of the Duke of Marlborough*, painted in the manner of a historical subject, was exhibited at the Royal Academy. Countless aristocrats posed for Reynolds, including the King and Queen, who were immortalized in his official portraits of them.

Now that paintings were an integral part of decorating a house, portraits and landscapes became the most popular subjects, particularly portraits, and any semi-talented artist who could paint in the style of the day could earn good money. William Hogarth was one of these, and although he came from humble beginnings, he was eventually able to amass a fortune. Hogarth could sense just what subjects would appeal to his clients, but at the same time he painted pictures that didn't spare society from his stinging criticism and satire.

In Master Hare, *as well as in other portraits of children, Reynolds displays a deep affinity for the gentle shapes and soft colors of childhood. Above, Reynolds paints a family portrait.*

Constable often does two versions of his landscapes, the sketches, which he draws on the site, and the work he completes in his studio. Although the spontaneous sketches contrast with the measured calm of the finished painting, his works reveal a freshness and a love of nature that herald a new era in painting. Seen here are The Water-Mill at Gillingham in Dorset (left), The Valley of the Stour (upper right) and Boat Building near Flatford Mill (lower right).

It was a style that in some ways anticipated modern painting.

On the other hand, John Constable did not achieve financial security until 1816 when he was forty and his father died, leaving him an inheritance. He did not marry the woman he loved until then either, because her parents were opposed to a man of no talent, so they thought, and no means. Although Constable is now regarded as the father of modern landscape painting, he did not reach his full artistic potential until late in life. His contribution lay in the way he discarded the concept of landscape as an idealized Paradise or a huge, theatrical setting, and portrayed the countryside just as it looked, with a naturalism that was combined with a feeling of real emotional involvement.

Both of Hogarth's paintings depict the aristocratic life. The Ball, top, is part of a moralizing series of paintings titled The Happy Marriage. The Performance, *bottom, is traditional, although even in this picture the children are portrayed as being mischievous and disobedient.*

The Decline of Venice

After the death of the extraordinary generation of painters who flourished in 16th-century Venice, 17th-century Venetian art became little more than a pale reflection of the new techniques that were being developed in the rest of Europe. And yet, during the century that followed, these distant echoes, set against the city's splendid artistic background, proved strong enough to inspire a number of major new talents, some as good as the Venetian painters who came before them. Although Venice was on the wane as a political power in the 18th century, even losing its status as an independent republic toward the end of the century, it experienced a revival of painting that resulted in a whole new series of masterpieces.

Three painters were responsible for this revival: Giambattista Tiepolo, Canaletto, and Francesco Guardi. Tiepolo's greatest works are found in churches, palaces and villas in Lombardy and the Veneto, the region that surrounds Venice. He is famous for his spectacularly painted ceilings, with their soaring luminous skies and their swirling masses of brilliantly foreshortened figures. He kept the colors in his paintings pale, with greens, pinks and blues predominant.

Tiepolo's fame spread rapidly, and he received commissions across Europe, from Germany to Spain. Because he was already fairly old when King Charles III invited him to come to Spain, he was accompanied by his sons, Lorenzo and Giandomenico, the latter a fine painter in his own right. Tiepolo died in Madrid in 1770, in an atmosphere that was increasingly hostile to his style of painting.

GIO. BTTA. TIEPOLO

In 1751 Tiepolo received an invitation from the Prince-Bishop of Würzburg to come to Germany to decorate his Residence with frescoes. The Würzburg frescoes, which are considered by many to be Tiepolo's finest work, include The Investiture of Bishop Harold, *shown here. Tiepolo produced hundreds of frescoes of this sort, partly because he painted small models from which assistants could carry out the work under his supervision.*

108

Guardi's two paintings hang in a Venetian palace on the
Grand Canal. Concert for the Counts of the North, *top,*
reflects the glittering Venetian life during the final
decades of the Republic. The Doge at the Church of the
Salute *hangs beneath it. Through the palace window, the
Church of Santa Maria della Salute can be seen on the
Grand Canal.*

At this time in Venice there was a vogue for paintings known as *vedute*, or views, whose subjects were almost always the city itself, or the water surrounding it. Francesco Guardi was particularly well known for this type of painting, although he did not confine himself completely to this one art form. His *vedute* possess a lively and animated quality and the details, rather than being clearly defined, shimmer in the light, with broken lines producing a quivery effect that recreates the dancing reflections of light from the water onto the surrounding scenery.

More accurate portrayals of Venice, with better geometrical perspective, are found in the *vedute* of Antonio Canal, known as Canaletto. Canaletto created his paintings of the city with the help of a *camera obscura*, a darkened mirror-lined box which had a small hole through which light could enter, thereby reproducing an upside-down image of the objects in front of it on a sheet of paper. By applying a lens to the hole, it was possible to see condensed images of wide panoramas. Although this *camera obscura* contained the basic principles of photography, Canaletto's pictures were not merely painted photographs. His sweeping panoramas of Venice, documented with precision, are lively glimpses of everyday life, and his scenes of Venice's many splendid festivals and ceremonies are bathed in a sharp, glowing light.

Canaletto enjoyed great success as a painter, not only in Venice, but also in England, where he traveled in 1746 and 1751.

Canaletto has just finished The Grand Canal and the
Bembo Palace, *a scene from mid-18th-century Venice.*

112

The Horrors of War

The French Revolution resulted in great political and social upheavals which were dramatically echoed in the lives and works of painters who lived through those troubled times. Both Goya and David, for instance, spent their last days in exile, which shows how much art, although primarily an individual means of expression, both interprets and is closely tied to politics and history. The subject matter the painter chooses, as well as his style, can be strongly influenced by the world around him.

Two events, a serious illness that led to deafness, and his war experiences, brought about a dramatic change in Goya's paintings. Goya, like Tiepolo, had had a difficult time having his work accepted, and his career in Madrid at the court of Charles III had progressed slowly. He had at first acquiesced to the tastes of the time which demanded dignity, simplicity and decorum.

Goya focuses all the light on the white shirt of the condemned man in The Third of May, 1808, *drawing attention to his desperate gesture of defiance, while the firing squad remains enveloped in gloom. The man is symbolic of the futility of killing men in war. In his outstretched hand you can see a little wound, identical to the mark left by a nail in the hand of Christ.*

114

After his illness, however, Goya's powers of observation sharpened, and he began to give full rein to his imagination. In a series of engravings known as *Caprices*, Goya attacked political corruption under Charles IV, who ascended the throne on the eve of the French Revolution. A few days after their publication, the engravings were withdrawn from sale, and Goya was taken into custody for questioning. Although he was finally released, he was forced to renounce his subversive work.

Goya was deeply moved by the conflict between Spain and France. When the French, under Napoleon, invaded Spain, the Spanish people strenuously resisted. On May 2, 1808, the people of Madrid rose up against the French invaders, but were gunned down in cold blood the following day. *The Second of May, 1808* and *The Third of May, 1808* are the titles of two famous paintings by Goya passionately depicting these events. Both graphic condemnations of useless violence, they are a total rejection of war and its atrocities. Goya later published a series of engravings entitled *Disasters of War* in which he portrayed with brutal realism his own dramatic impressions and feelings of anguish.

After the downfall of Napoleon, the monarchy was restored in Spain and, again, anyone who expressed even remotely liberal ideas was savagely suppressed. In 1819, a deaf and unwell Goya retired to the countryside to his house called Quinta del Sordo (House of the Deaf Man), where he painted disturbing paintings that reveal an obsessive, almost nightmarish quality. Finally, for his own safety, he retreated into voluntary exile in the French city of Bordeaux.

Goya has had a tremendous influence on modern painting, and all the major painters in the great artistic movements of the 19th and 20th centuries have admired and studied his work.

Jacques-Louis David's Napoleon Crossing the Alps *is an example of how portraits of Napoleon often suffer from heroic exaggeration.*

Even before the French Revolution, Jacques-Louis David was widely acclaimed for bringing the world of Greco-Roman antiquity to life by painting mythological and historical scenes with precision and feeling. He had lived in Rome for five years studying firsthand both the works of classical antiquity and the great masters of 16th-century Italy.

Although King Louis XVI himself expressed interest in David's work, as a member of the Revolutionary Assembly, David was soon voting for the monarch's death. But when his friend Robespierre, the Revolutionary leader, fell from power, David too was imprisoned. During Napoleon's rise to First Consul and then to Emperor, David dedicated his art to Bonaparte's greater glory, and dominated French painting through the Empire period. In 1816, after the fall of Napoleon and the restoration of the monarchy, David was exiled to Brussels where he continued to paint until his death in 1825.

During the Napoleonic Wars, free passage of artists and works of art through European countries was halted. Neither the Frenchman J.-B.-Camille Corot nor the Englishman Joseph M.W. Turner was able to visit Italy until the second decade of the 19th century, when they both made trips that had significant effects on their artistic development.

Corot enjoyed great success in France. His neatly designed landscapes had a well-defined sense of space which appealed to Neoclassical tastes, while the grayish-white light he preferred gave them a nostalgic quality which appealed to the Romantics.

Part of Turner's success was actually due to the war between England and France: Because there was no trade between the two countries, the English aristocracy's demand for paintings had to be filled by home-grown artists.

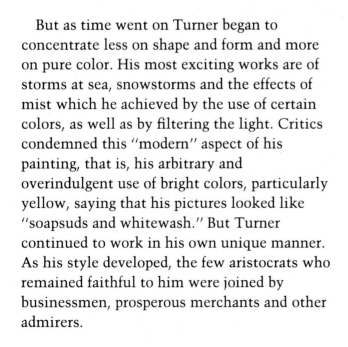

But as time went on Turner began to concentrate less on shape and form and more on pure color. His most exciting works are of storms at sea, snowstorms and the effects of mist which he achieved by the use of certain colors, as well as by filtering the light. Critics condemned this "modern" aspect of his painting, that is, his arbitrary and overindulgent use of bright colors, particularly yellow, saying that his pictures looked like "soapsuds and whitewash." But Turner continued to work in his own unique manner. As his style developed, the few aristocrats who remained faithful to him were joined by businessmen, prosperous merchants and other admirers.

It was Corot versus Turner, just as it was France versus England in the wars that took place in the artists' lifetimes. Corot was shy and retiring, while Turner was adventurous and self-assured. These differences can be seen in their landscapes of similar subjects, Corot's Castelgandolfo, *left, and Turner's* Crossing the Brook, *right. Turner's "hot" colors were inspired by his travels to Italy, where they were necessary to capture the Mediterranean light. Corot, on the other hand, instead of a range of colors, used shades of the same color. He painted hundreds of pictures which were so popular that many fakes were produced to satisfy the demand. It has been said that Corot painted 1000 pictures, 1500 of which are in Britain and America.*

119

The Establishment and the Romantic Movement

During the 19th century, art became the subject of heated discussions, with scholars and philosophers joining the fray, as artists banded together in groups, each group advocating a particular style. As art criticism appeared in journals and learned papers, aesthetics, the theory of art criticism, was born. Paris was the center of these new artistic ideas, and it was mainly French painters who provided the answers to the burning artistic questions of the day. Every year an official exhibition was held in

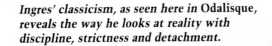

Ingres' classicism, as seen here in Odalisque, reveals the way he looks at reality with discipline, strictness and detachment.

the *Salon* (a large gallery in the Louvre Museum in Paris), where a jury would grade and award prizes to new works of art.

During this period, the styles of two French painters, Ingres and Delacroix, stood in direct opposition to one another. Ingres, who was a pupil of David's, kept the traditions of Classical art alive, while Delacroix headed up the Romantic movement. Many believed that a good deal of Ingres' work was carried out as a kind of duel with Delacroix, and, as a matter of fact, many of their pictures were exhibited opposite each other in the annual Salons.

Ingres, who lived in Italy for long periods, found his ideal in the classical serenity of Raphael, rather than in the tension of Michelangelo or the dramatic light and shade of Caravaggio, both of whom appealed to the Romantics. Ingres believed in clarity and precision of line along with a simple and coherent treatment of space. The political implications of Neoclassicism, which had been associated with Napoleon and the French Revolution, held no appeal for Ingres, who continued to search for artistic perfection well beyond the Empire period, right up until the time of his death in 1867.

Because portraiture does not call for any deep psychological interpretation, it is an ideal subject for Ingres who has here captured beautiful Marie-Françoise Beauregard Rivière at her most richly costumed. Ingres, who loves music, is also a talented violinist.

121

Courbet's monumental work Burial at Ornans *is the embodiment of realistic painting, with life-size figures depicting the burial of a peasant in Ornans, where Courbet came from.*

In 1819, the French painter Théodore Géricault exhibited his *Raft of the Medusa* at the Louvre. The canvas depicted a historical event, the mutiny and shipwreck of the French frigate *Medusa* off the African coast, leaving her desperate survivors clinging to a raft. The public had been deeply aroused by the tragic incident, and the delay in rescuing the survivors had caused a bitter controversy in the government. The painting incited controversy too. The press declared it a scandal, while the young painters of the day saw it as the final nail in the coffin that sealed the fate of David's Neoclassical school of painting. The famous Socialist philosopher Pierre Joseph Proudhon, who favored Géricault's painting, later remarked that one painting like the *Raft of the Medusa* could redeem a whole gallery filled with Madonnas, odalisques and idealizations.

Géricault's early death at the age of thirty-three strengthened his reputation, and he was claimed not only by the Classicists, among whom he had received his early training, but also by the Romantics such as Delacroix, who mourned him as a master. Actually, his work contained elements from both schools. In the *Raft of the Medusa*, Géricault borrowed the design of the picture and the anatomy of the bodies from the Classical school. From the Romantic school he borrowed the movement into a background and the subject.

Gustave Courbet, who was born in 1819, the year the *Medusa* was shown, devoted his life to the realities of contemporary politics and

society. It is known that Courbet greatly admired Géricault's *Raft of the Medusa* and it was Géricault's accurate portrayal of a real event that was the basis for Courbet's whole philosophy of painting, which he went on to develop in works such as *Burial at Ornans*.

To avoid a scandal similar to the one created when the *Medusa* was exhibited, Courbet's *Burial at Ornans* was not allowed to be shown at the 1855 Universal Exposition in Paris. In protest, Courbet withdrew all his other works and held a show of his own in what he called a Pavilion of Realism. Courbet was one of a new breed, both as a man and as an artist. Although the newspapers and Romantic painters referred to his bad taste and vulgarity, for the first time an artist was showing the common people as they really were, without pity or poetry.

Courbet was active in the political upheavals that resulted in the formation of the Paris Commune in 1870. Because he was accused of demolishing the column which commemorated Napoleon in the Place Vendôme, he was thrown in prison and finally forced into exile.

Tens of thousands of people flock to see Géricault's* Raft of the Medusa *in London and Dublin, its popularity more than compensating for its failure to win a prize in Paris.

123

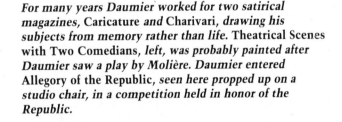

For many years Daumier worked for two satirical magazines, Caricature *and* Charivari, *drawing his subjects from memory rather than life.* Theatrical Scenes with Two Comedians, *left, was probably painted after Daumier saw a play by Molière. Daumier entered* Allegory of the Republic, *seen here propped up on a studio chair, in a competition held in honor of the Republic.*

Honoré Daumier created a true human comedy in his four thousand lithographs, just like the human comedy his contemporary Honoré de Balzac was creating in his novels. Although he had spent six months in prison for creating a caricature of King Louis Philippe as Gargantua, Daumier continued to paint critical satires of the men who enforced the oppressive laws of his day. His sympathies lay with the common people, and he participated in the revolution which overthrew Louis Philippe and led to the formation of the Republic in 1848, the same year that he painted *Allegory of the Republic.* Daumier was again at the barricades in 1870 during the period of the Paris Commune.

Because Daumier, who began his career as an amateur, was basically self-taught, he remained outside the conventional mainstream of art and consequently developed his own free and personal style. Since he was not considered an important painter, only six of his works were exhibited in the official Salon, and although a few critics appreciated his efforts, he sold very few works, and those mostly among his own friends. As a result, he lived and died in poverty, with not even his wife believing in his talent. When he died, she sold all of his possessions for almost nothing—his paints, paintings, drawings, easels. It was not until decades later that Daumier's art was considered important and the lessons to be learned from it came to be appreciated.

Eugène Delacroix wanted to be regarded as representative of all serious 19th-century painting, but in his time he was generally regarded as the leading Romantic painter, just as he is today. Although he considered himself to be a modern painter, Delacroix did not believe that meant a complete break with the past, and his ideal was Michelangelo and the way Michelangelo endowed his figures with a feeling of movement and emotion. Delacroix also admired Rubens, from whom he derived his sense of color and lively composition. As a matter of fact, it was these very characteristics which lay at the heart of Romantic painting.

Delacroix was an intellectual who corresponded and argued with his colleagues and critics, mostly through his extensive activities as an artist. He left some 850 oil paintings and more than 1500 works in pastel, watercolor and ink, thousands of drawings and dozens of albums full of sketches, together with a series of murals commissioned by highly placed government officials as well as by the King himself. Delacroix was socially popular, and although he was attracted by the exciting notion of mounting the barricades in the name of freedom, he felt more comfortable in the wealthy drawing rooms of Paris.

Few other artists of his time were presented with so many opportunities to shine. Delacroix rose to the challenge and excelled.

Delacroix brought back many ideas for paintings from his travels in Morocco and Algeria in 1832. Women of Algiers immortalizes an Arabian harem which Delacroix visited in Algiers.

Impressionism

In 1874, a group of painters held an exhibit of their works in the studio of an important Parisian photographer of the day, Paul Nadar. The show, which made a clean break with the Classical and Romantic conventions of the past, produced violently negative criticism. Renoir, Degas, Cézanne, Pissarro, Sisley and Monet were the most important members of this group, and it was because of Monet's *Impression, Sunrise* that they became derisively known as Impressionists. Undaunted, they took the name for themselves and the following year held a sale of the "Impressionists" which the public attended strictly as a form of entertainment.

These artistic revolutionaries not only rejected the official art of the Salons, but also rejected traditional techniques, the arranging and lighting of models in a studio, preparatory drawings and working with light and shade. Because they perceived shapes as being defined by the juxtaposition of color, they did not feel the need to work with preparatory drawings. Black was eliminated, light and shade being achieved by using different colors rather than by darkening the basic tone. Their canvases were, for instance, famous for their mauve shadows.

Although Edouard Manet was never part of the group and showed his paintings, when they were accepted, in the official Salons, he was an immediate forerunner of Impressionism. *Déjeuner sur l'herbe* and *Olympia* especially anticipated Impressionism, although *Olympia* enraged viewers

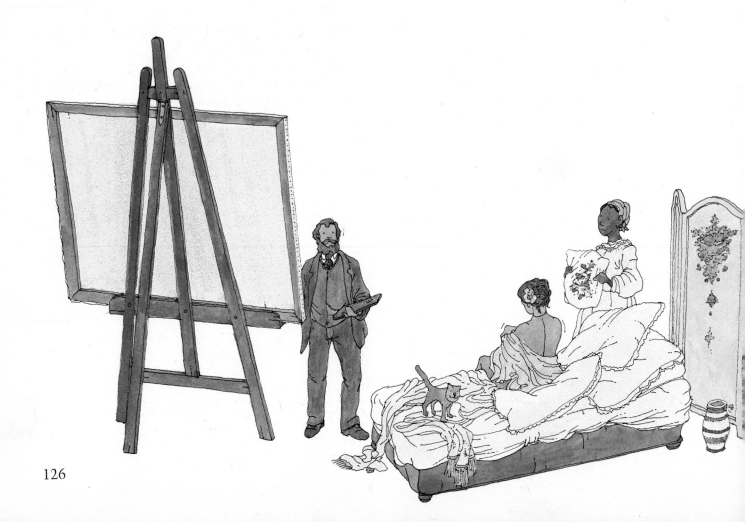

when it was exhibited at the Salon in 1865. Manet was no revolutionary in his private life, but a well-to-do member of the middle class whose greatest ambition was to have his paintings officially accepted. He was also a passionate student of art from the past, and the subjects of both *Déjeuner sur l'herbe* and *Olympia* were taken from well-known earlier works.

Olympia was an updated interpretation of the Venuses of Titian, Velazquez and Goya, with a rather well-known Parisian girl as the model. In the same manner, *Déjeuner sur l'herbe* was a transformation of Giorgione's *Fête Champêtre* into a picnic among friends. It was this very "desecration" of the classics that infuriated Manet's critics. In reply, Manet asserted that a painter must belong to his own time and paint what he sees around him.

It was not until 1881 that Manet won a second prize at the Salon, and it was not until after his death in 1883 that his works were sold, and that their value began to rise. His great contribution lay in his role as the godfather, so to speak, of modern painting.

When Manet's Olympia *is exhibited, viewers are so outraged that it has to be hung out of reach for fear of damage. Although both traditional artists and realists consider it proper to portray the female body idealistically rather than realistically, the young artists who want to break away from all established rules and create an alternative kind of art are electrified by Manet's work.*

Just as the introduction of the mechanical loom affected the work of the weaver, so the invention of photography in 1839 took over much of the painter's documentary work, portraits, illustrations and plates for books and journals. But painting offers something unique: It can investigate reality to a greater extent than photography. For instance, it can add thought and emotion to a portrait, or introduce movement and variation to a landscape. Once people became aware that painting and photography were two different artistic and technical means of expression, no further comparisons were made, and a relationship of mutual interest developed between the two.

The Impressionists, who declared that they were in favor of realism, concentrated on finding new ways to capture reality. Monet, Renoir and Sisley would often go to the banks of the Seine together, not to make sketches that they would reproduce later in their studios, but to paint "on location," using splashes of color that would give a sense of immediacy to their impressions of water, sky and sun. Because they now interpreted depth of vision with different shades of color, and because details would not be noticed in a sweeping glance, they were no longer faced with the problems of perspective or the portrayal of minute detail. With this new technique, they sought to "see" the countryside, not copy it; capture the feelings of the person looking at nature and not the feel of nature itself.

As Impressionist visions, Claude Monet's landscapes have never been surpassed. He depicted not only the visual reality of the countryside, but also his own state of mind, as in the *Regatta at Argenteuil*. The garden in the background of this painting was the one at Monet's house in Argenteuil on the Seine, where he and his family moved in 1872. Manet came to visit him here, and together with Renoir, the three sometimes painted in the garden.

Monet, who painted the Regatta at Argenteuil *out of doors*, has perhaps stepped away from his easel to talk to Manet and Renoir who have come to visit him.

Impressionism developed through lively and continual discussions within its own ranks. Members of the movement were diverse, held strong opinions, and often disagreed vehemently with one another. Actually the movement did not last very long, with its last collective exhibition held in 1886, only twelve years after its first.

The dancers in the foreground of Degas' The Dance Lesson, *left, are not the center of attention. Instead, in typical Degas fashion, the eye is led diagonally from above, as if looking on from the wings of a theater.*

The shadows around the orchestra in Degas' The Orchestra at the Opera, *below, contrast to the light and life of the dancers on the stage. This picture, too, is painted at an original angle usually associated with photography.*

Although Monet and Renoir tended to use a purely visual technique, Degas' concept of painting involved not only the eye but also the mind. Degas, who belonged to Manet's generation, was older than the others, and because he had pursued regular academic studies, he never gave up the solid spatial composition of his scenes. What was new about his painting, however, was the way he viewed his scenes from unusual angles, in an almost detached way, a technique he may have picked up from photography, which interested him greatly. But photography captures a precise moment and freezes it in mid-movement, whereas Degas tried to capture a movement in its entirety.

Although Monet and Renoir preferred to paint outside in order to catch the play of light as they saw it, Degas painted interiors, particularly the theater, with its artificial lights. Because of his interest in movement, dance especially appealed to him, and his unique scenes of ballerinas absorbed in the expressive poses and gestures of the ballet world have become universally famous.

Degas also distinguished himself by using less dazzling colors than the other Impressionists, partly so that he could better reflect the sad and harsh aspects of the Parisian life he was portraying. His personal artistic quest led to his almost total isolation, an isolation that was heightened by his increasing blindness toward the end of his life. During those later years, Degas did a good deal of modeling in wax.

Him, Her and the Dog
Henri de Toulouse-Lautrec

Blue Vase
Paul Cézanne

High Tide at Port-en-Bressin
Georges Seurat

The Saint-Martin Canal
Alfred Sisley

Card Players
Paul Cézanne

Argenteuil
Edouard Manet

Haymaking in Brittany
Paul Gauguin

Portrait of Marguerite Gachet
Vincent Van Gogh

Entrance to the Village of Voisins
Camille Pissarro

Here, in an imaginary art gallery hung with famous paintings, it is obvious that despite similarities, each artist has his own distinguishing style. Seurat breaks colors down into primary components, laying on dots of pure color in order to build up variations of tone. Sisley is concerned with images reflected in water. Cézanne's reality has a more substantial, concrete form. Gauguin and Van Gogh share a poetic view of the world. Pissarro faithfully portrays the details of his subject matter.

Two artists stand out on their own within the Impressionist movement: Van Gogh and Toulouse-Lautrec.

Vincent Van Gogh discovered his vocation for painting rather late in life, after a series of personal misfortunes that combined to depress and isolate him. His compassion for the poor and oppressed had led him, in a sudden burst of generosity, to give away everything he owned to the poor, resulting in his own desperate poverty. Van Gogh produced eight hundred paintings, as well as hundreds of drawings, only one of which he sold.

In painting, Van Gogh found a way to communicate his thoughts and feelings to others. He aimed to go beyond the pure vision of reality of the Impressionists by introducing a moral element into his work. Nevertheless, it was from meeting and associating with Impressionist painters when he went to Paris to live with his brother in 1886 that Van Gogh drew inspiration for his art, and all his most important works date

Working in the fields is a recurrent theme in Van Gogh's paintings. In the life-like and poetic Peasants Enjoying a Siesta, *left, every line radiates feeling.*

Van Gogh's Room at Arles, *right, provides a glimpse of the so-called Yellow House in Arles where Van Gogh lived in isolation.*

Toulouse-Lautrec draws The Washerwoman, *left, a typical character from the Montmartre district of Paris.* Moorish Dance, *right, is for a wall panel in a Parisian cabaret.*

from that time. Van Gogh spent four years in France, staying two years in Paris, and then visiting Arles in the south of France. While in Arles he suffered bouts of depression which resulted in a stay in a psychiatric hospital. Following his return to Paris, he committed suicide at the age of thirty-seven.

Like Van Gogh, Henri de Toulouse-Lautrec spent his life in a frenzy of work, and he too died at thirty-seven. As a child, Toulouse-Lautrec broke both his legs in an accident which left him crippled for life. Although he was an aristocrat by birth, he haunted the dance halls, cafés, variety theaters and the circus of Paris. His studio was in Montmartre, a district of Paris famous for its night life, and it was there, at their places of work, that he painted entertainers, singers, dancers and clowns.

Toulouse-Lautrec, who made use of a form of printing known as lithography, produced works with sweeping areas of pure color and no shading. He used this technique in the posters he created for theatrical shows and exhibitions, such as his famous posters for the Moulin Rouge cabaret. Although he was the first painter associated with advertising, he produced his posters with the same attention to detail he gave to his paintings.

In 1899 heavy drinking forced Toulouse-Lautrec to enter a sanatorium, where he died two years later. A museum was dedicated to him in his hometown of Albi, displaying the collection of works that were found in his studio.

Renoir's **Dance at the Moulin de la Galette,** *depicting people gathered for a Sunday dance, is a celebration of youth and life.*

Auguste Renoir, along with Monet, was an originator of the painting style composed of atmosphere, color and pure form that is known as early Impressionism. Nevertheless, in order to embark on his own personal voyage of artistic discovery, Renoir was the first to break away from the group that had held their famous exhibition in Nadar's photography studio.

Renoir, who had studied art from an early age, exhibited in the official Salons of 1864 and 1865. During the next two years, however, his works were rejected, and becoming increasingly irritated by the academic atmosphere of the Salons, he began to realize that the fixed rules of traditional painting were too restrictive. After 1867, he began to spend some time each year painting outdoors at Fontainebleau with one or another of his artist friends, and it was during this time that he experimented with his painting, a move that ultimately led him to Impressionism.

Dance at the Moulin de la Galette was a masterpiece of Renoir's new style. The figures were no longer physical objects in a set of surroundings, but apparitions generated by the atmosphere of those surroundings. Light playing tricks with colors: This was what created the figures and made them move. The actual subject was of little importance, while the shape itself, created by color alone, was primarily a product of the painting process. Renoir's skill lay in his ability to place different shades of color side by side, ranging from the brightest to the softest so that they enhanced each other without destroying the overall harmony.

Renoir quickly sensed that he had exhausted all the possibilities of this technique, and declared that he no longer knew either how to draw or how to paint. This crisis sent him into the artistic past: He traveled to Italy where he rediscovered Raphael and Tiepolo, and also studied the works of Delacroix. But as the basis for new experiments in his work, Renoir turned to the paintings of Ingres, the master of this style of pure beauty. Renoir sought new techniques by continuing to work on his paintings, not just by formulating abstract theories.

Impressionism was not a school of painting with rules and regulations, but a group of artists who brought about a revolution in painting by means of their own works. Because of this freedom, and because of the inspiration the members gave each other without traditional master-pupil relationships, Impressionism produced many outstanding artists who in turn created many great paintings.

Baigneuses (Women Bathing) expresses Renoir's rediscovery of the balance between classical composition and Impressionist techniques.

Fauves and Cubists

Criticism of Impressionism's purely visual character erupted within the group itself and not only led to its breakup, but brought about the birth of new artistic groups as well. It was no longer important to portray the external impression; now what mattered was the forceful, sometimes violent expression of inner reality. As a result of this new impetus, two Expressionist movements were born, the Fauves ("wild beasts") in France and Die Brücke ("the bridge") in Germany.

The aim of the Fauves was to transform reality; they used a familiar outline, such as a figure, as an area for experimenting with different, explosively applied bands of glowing colors. The Fauves were testing the bounds of reality without going to the extreme of abstraction. Henri Matisse was the central figure of the Fauve movement, while the young Pablo Picasso kept a somewhat critical distance. But when Picasso did arrive on the scene, it was to introduce a revolutionary new art movement called Cubism. At this point the Fauves movement was over.

Gypsy Woman
Henri Matisse

Paddock at Deauville
Raoul Dufy

Matisse's figures are powerfully shaped by violent color as form becomes content as well. Painting now has a reality in its own right, independent of visual reality, so that it is no longer a question of reproduction, but of re-creation.

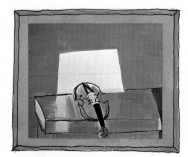

The Red Violin
Raoul Dufy

In Dufy's works, color, divorced from the effects of light, is all, even the basic outline becoming a matter of the artist's personal choice.

Cubism was concerned solely with reality in the everyday domestic world. But rather than illustrating it realistically, as Courbet had done, the Cubists introduced a new dimension, time. A Cubist picture provided simultaneous, meticulously detailed representations of objects viewed from different angles or in different stages of movement.

Still Life with Score by Satie
Georges Braque

Still Life with Playing Cards
Georges Braque

Although Braque was one of the leading Fauve painters, he later turned to Cubism. Paintings are no longer a screen on which figures are projected, but a surface on which they are broken down and reassembled.

Women in a Room
Fernand Léger

Homage to Louis David
Fernand Léger

Léger, who is a great believer in the Age of the Machine, creates a mythical, mechanical world as he strives for a new, monumental style of painting.

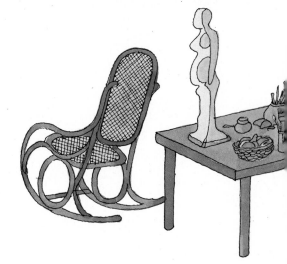

*Picasso's immense black-and-white painting Guernica
depicts the aerial bombardment in 1936 of Guernica, an
unarmed Basque village, during the Spanish civil war.
The nightmarish quality of the painting, with its antiwar
message, is a burning indictment of violence and
politically repressive regimes, as the large figures bathed
in a ghostly light scream their despair in a final act of
protest. For a long time the painting hung in the
Museum of Modern Art in New York. It was restored to
Spain only after that country returned to democracy.*

Pablo Picasso, the son of a Spanish artist who was also a professor at the
Barcelona Academy, moved to Paris in 1903 at the age of twenty-two.
Although he was familiar with Impressionism and the Fauves, in his early
work he revealed a figurative tendency which was allied to a socially aware
and poetic sense of realism. Picasso also painted poor people, circus people,
theatrical people, all with a clear, strong sense of line in a single color, first
blue, then gray, and then pink. His choice of subject and color was in stark
opposition to the Fauves, whom Picasso viewed as mere imitators of the
Impressionists.

Between 1906 and 1910, Picasso, together with a fellow Cubist, Georges Braque, experimented with a new way to portray space and reality. They dismantled surfaces and depicted several views of a single object at the same time. In 1907, Picasso painted *Les Demoiselles d'Avignon*, in which he introduced his own interpretation of certain elements in primitive African art. This history-making painting, which marked the moment when the break was made with all the art of the past, is now considered to be the universal symbol of Cubism.

It was Matisse who unwittingly coined the word Cubism in his criticism of a painting by Braque which he attacked as being built out of endless little cubes. Actually, the geometrical style of Cubist painting in some ways did justify this description, and the name stuck. Soon other artists joined Braque and Picasso, and because some of them were gifted, the new style became a subject for serious consideration, once that first shock had worn off. After 1910, Cubist exhibitions were organized in Paris, as well as in the other major capitals of Europe and in New York. These shows not only aroused interest, but they also provoked extreme and frequently hostile reactions. "Evil" and "outrageous" were a few of the milder words used to describe them.

After World War I, Picasso began to branch out in different directions. He returned to figurative art, studying the famous works of 19th-century French painters and interpreting them in a personal way. Picasso, who alternated between naturalistic and highly abstract paintings, also worked in graphics, sculpture and ceramics, all with an inventiveness and

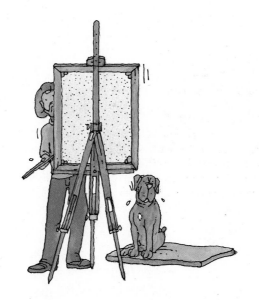

technical ability that made him seem to be an artistic god.

As time went on, Picasso not only became the yardstick by which all other artists were judged, but also the sole arbiter of artistic activity in Paris. He continued to produce works of art with amazing vitality and consistency right up until the final months of his long life.

STYLES AND PERIODS

BYZANTINE

There is a vast body of Western European art created between the 6th and 13th centuries that is known as Byzantine. These works show the influence of artists from the Eastern Roman Empire whose capital was Byzantium (Constantinople), as well as the influence of eastern Mediterranean artists. The Byzantine style was characterized by the icon, a religious picture of stylized figures in fixed poses whose expressions show great spirituality. Although the main center of Byzantine art was Ravenna, Italy, fine examples were also produced in Venice and Rome, as well as in Tuscany, where Byzantine art flourished right up until the time of Cimabue and Duccio.

ROMANESQUE

Romanesque art, which developed in the 8th century and reached its height in the 11th and 12th centuries, was the first of two great international styles of medieval Western European art. The Romanesque style derived from a meeting of the Roman Christian tradition, and the so-called barbarian cultures of northern Europe. In painting, its highest forms of expression were the miniature (the decoration of illuminated manuscripts and gospels) and frescoes (decorations of the walls of churches and chapels). Two famous artists, Cimabue and Giotto, were both Romanesque painters.

GOTHIC

Fifteenth-century artists of the Italian Renaissance condemned the architecture of the preceding two centuries by calling it Gothic, meaning that the Goths, a barbarian tribe from Northern Europe, had destroyed the art of the Roman Empire. Following a reevaluation of the art of this period, particularly by 19th-century art critics, Gothic has lost its derogatory meaning.

Gothic art, with its strong religious overtones, developed around the mid-12th century in northern France, and from there spread throughout Europe lasting right up until the 16th century in northern Europe. In Italy its main spheres of development were in the northern and central regions, although it was replaced during the 15th century by the new trends of the Renaissance and consequently was a short-lived movement.

Because Gothic art expressed the world of chivalry and courtly love, it was particularly favored in the noble courts of the 14th century. The Gothic style, characterized by gentle shapes, pure and harmonious lines, and pale, delicate colors, was popularized by miniatures, which achieved a remarkable degree of stylistic consistency throughout Europe. Simone Martini and Gentile da Fabriano in Italy, and Rogier van der Weyden in Flanders, were all Gothic painters.

RENAISSANCE

Renaissance art, which was essentially an Italian phenomenon covering the 15th and 16th centuries, gradually replaced the linear style of Gothic art. The rediscovery of the Greco-Roman world, which centered on man and his life on earth, led to a revival of interest in humanist ideals, as well as in the study of man's basic qualities and history.

In painting, the scene was dominated by the human figure, which the artist brought into relief by the skillful use of light. The figure's surroundings were carefully drawn to scale, with all elements portrayed in perfect proportion by means of perspective. This new art style spread from Tuscany to all of Italy, and from there it filtered through the rest of Europe. In Venice it acquired a unique quality with a special emphasis placed on the use of color.

MANNERISM

In the late 16th century, painters known as Mannerists saw Michelangelo's flouting of Renaissance tradition with his *Last Judgment* (1541) as a signal to break away from the rigid formalism of the kind of Renaissance art that was typified by the perfection of Raphael. The Mannerists wanted to indulge in a freer, more complex, and less static type of composition. Although Mannerism was never popular in Venice, it was essentially an Italian movement, with the greatest Mannerist painters being Pontormo, Parmigianino and Bronzino.

BAROQUE

After the uncertainty of Mannerism, a wave of confidence and vitality returned with the Baroque, a style that was characteristic of 17th-century court and religious art. It abandoned the balance and proportions of Renaissance art in favor of lively colors and much stronger emotional content. The style was at its purest in the work of Bernini, Caravaggio and the late Rubens from 1630 to 1680 when it was known as High Baroque and virtually confined to Rome. In the 18th century, Baroque, which had become more delicate and decorative, was known as Rococo.

NEOCLASSICISM

At the end of the 18th century, people began to react against the rather tired and formalized excesses of the Baroque and Rococo styles. They felt the need to return to the planned simplicity and linear purity of the Greco-Roman, or Classical, art as it was interpreted by the Italian Renaissance. From 1748 on, the discoveries of the ruins of Pompeii and Herculaneum gave impetus to this feeling. The supporters of this movement, which was known as Neoclassicism, began to dominate the art academies as they attempted to impose strict artistic rules and guidelines. The founder of Neoclassicism was Jacques-Louis David, whose pupil Ingres carried the Neoclassicist standard into battle against the Romantic movement of the 1820s.

ROMANTICISM

Neoclassicism, to some, was too cold and rigid. It seemed unable to express man's feelings, tensions and dramas. The Romantic movement called not only for the revival of the Classical world, but also of the Gothic, with particular emphasis on a return to nature. The Romantics detested the restriction of Neoclassicism, creating elaborate and complex works instead, often using dark colors. The two greatest Romantic painters were Géricault and Delacroix.

REALISM

Both Neoclassicism and Romanticism provided moral and aesthetic interpretations of the world without dealing with pure reality. The Realist movement, which developed during the second half of the 19th century, remained aloof from the arguments between Neoclassicists and Romantics. It proposed instead the portrayal of social reality, such as the everyday life of the peasant as it really was, unrefined, often sordid, but spontaneous. The French painter Courbet was the embodiment of Realism.

IMPRESSIONISM

Rather than being an aesthetic movement which dealt with the theory of art, Impressionism was the product of a group of artists who developed a new technique of painting that owed nothing to conventional artistic rules. The Impressionists, using Realism as their starting point, tried to capture the actual sensation of seeing, with all its elements of light and color. Because the group included a number of different and often conflicting artistic personalities, it broke up before the end of the 19th century.

CUBISM

At the beginning of the 1900s, a revolutionary new artistic movement called Cubism was born. Sparked mainly by Picasso, painting no longer *just* represented reality, but now created new shapes and forms as well, based on the examination of everyday objects that had been dismantled and viewed from several different angles.

LIVES OF THE GREAT PAINTERS

ALBRECHT ALTDORFER (c. 1480–1538)

Albrecht Altdorfer, who was born in Bavaria, traveled to Regensburg in 1505 with his father Ulrich, a painter. There he gained a considerable reputation, becoming city architect and councillor.

Because he painted so many landscapes, it is often assumed he was a great traveler, but his only known journey was to Venice in 1535. Altdorfer, who endowed Regensburg with a number of important buildings and fortifications, has always been known for his landscapes, not as settings for human figures, but as subjects in their own right.

ANDREA DEL CASTAGNO (c. 1423–1457)

Andrea di Bartolo di Bargella owed his name to the village of Castagno, near Florence, Italy, where he was born. He moved to Florence at an early age, and at only seventeen was commissioned to paint the likenesses of rebels who had risen up against the Medici and been put to death after the battle of Anghiari. As a result of this commission, Andrea was nicknamed Andreino degli Impiccati, "Andreino of the hanged men."

After a brief stay in Venice, Castagno returned to Florence to undertake his greatest artistic project, painting the frescoes in the refectory of the Convent of Sant' Apollonia, depicting the *Last Supper, Crucifixion, Deposition* and *Resurrection*. He is also known for his paintings *Famous Men and Women*, as well as his last work, a fresco portrait of the military leader Niccolò da Tolentino in Florence Cathedral. Castagno, whose painting style was highly original, enclosed his figures in hard vigorous lines which conveyed a strong sense of realism.

FRA ANGELICO (c. 1400–1455)

Guido di Pietro, who was born at Vicchio in Mugello, near Florence, worked as a youth on illuminated manuscripts, achieving a high degree of elegance and refinement in both line and color. When he entered the Dominican order of friars, he took the name Fra Giovanni da Fiesole, although after his death he was given the name Angelico, with the word Beato (Blessed) added. Certainly the beautiful spiritual quality that shines through his work has justified his name.

Of fundamental importance to Fra Angelico's development as an artist was his collaboration with the famous architect Michelozzi, who was commissioned by Cosimo de' Medici to rebuild the Dominican convent of St. Mark's in Florence. With Michelozzi designing the airy and linear architecture, Fra Angelico carried out all the fresco decoration. In line with the artistic ideas of the early Renaissance, Fra Angelico introduced clear perspective into his paintings of architecture, while also retaining the gracefulness of the late Gothic tradition. The frescoes, in which his figures show a sense of color unequaled by his contemporaries, took Fra Angelico from 1437 to 1446 to complete, after which he was summoned to Rome by Pope Eugenius IV and Pope Nicholas V to carry out various projects. The only surviving work from these years in Rome are the frescoes in the Chapel of Nicholas V depicting the lives of St. Stephen and St. Lawrence. Other outstanding works by Fra Angelico are his *Coronation of the Virgin* and *Annunciation*.

ANTONELLO DA MESSINA (c. 1430–1479)

It is believed that Antonello da Messina, the only major southern Italian painter of the 15th century, was born in Messina, Sicily. Receiving his early training in Naples, Antonello was the only Italian artist to be decisively influenced by the precise oil technique associated with the van Eycks. Although he adopted the meticulous technique and analytical naturalism of this Flemish tradition, he also drew from the simple, clearly defined perspective of the Florentine Renaissance. Antonello worked in Venice for only about two years, but he produced some of his most memorable paintings there such as his *Crucifixion* and *St. Sebastian*, and his style had a great influence on Venetian painting. In September of 1476 Antonello returned to his birthplace, Messina, where he painted his great *Annunciation* and *Portrait of a Man*. It was in Messina that he died in 1479.

THE BELLINI

Jacopo Bellini, who was born in Venice, Italy, around 1400 and died there in 1470, dominated the contemporary Venetian art scene, along with his sons Gentile and Giovanni. Jacopo was a pupil of Gentile da Fabriano, in whose honor he named one of his own sons. Despite his links to the Late Gothic tradition of the Venetian region, Jacopo was receptive to the innovations introduced to Venice and Padua by Early Renaissance Tuscan painters. Although few of Jacopo's works have survived, he left two important books of drawings to his painter sons.

Gentile Bellini, who was born in Venice about 1429, was a great draftsman with an elegant and meticulous style. Gentile not only worked with his father and brother, but he was also chosen to travel to Constantinople when Sultan Mahommet II requested the Doge to send him an outstanding painter. Gentile died in Venice in 1507.

Jacopo's most important artistic heir was Giovanni, born around 1430. Also known as Giambellino, Giovanni succeeded in going beyond the prevailing Late Gothic tradition by introducing natural realism and settings of majestic serenity, the very elements that characterized Renaissance painting. For this reason, the Bellini brothers' contacts with their brother-in-law, Andrea Mantegna, were of great importance, although Giovanni rejected Mantegna's harshness of design and his taste for the grandiose and the antique. Giovanni preferred a gentler and more tranquil style, combined with a use of light and color that paved the way for the colorism which typified the work of later Venetian painters. In his more than sixty years as an artist, Giovanni created masterpieces in portraiture, religious painting and even profane art, such as *The Feast of the Gods*, which Titian completed after Giovanni's death in 1516.

SANDRO BOTTICELLI (c. 1445–1510)

Botticelli, whose real name was Alessandro Filipepi, lived and worked in Florence, Italy, at the time of Lorenzo the Magnificent, when the Medici court was at its most powerful. Botticelli, who was one of the most original painters of the 15th century, was in close contact with the philosophers and scholars who flourished at the Medici court. As a result of this intellectual atmosphere, he produced such great allegorical works as *Spring* and *The Birth of Venus*.

Botticelli was invited to Rome in 1481 to collaborate on the biblical frescoes for the Sistine Chapel. While working there, he became acquainted with classical art, which inspired him to paint with a greater sense of compositional balance and strength. By 1500, however, his style was so obviously in opposition to the mainstream of Leonardo and Michelangelo that his immense popularity began to wane.

Deeply moved by the preaching of Savonarola, Botticelli devoted the last ten years of his life to painting large religious works. There is a continual vein of melancholy running through all of Botticelli's paintings, and even his Venuses seem to embody an earthly, human beauty that never completely matches the ideals of absolute beauty.

GEORGES BRAQUE (1882–1963)

Like Dufy, Georges Braque studied at night school in Le Havre, having been born in Argenteuil, France. Although he was originally attracted to the Fauves in Paris, he was soon drawn to the more concrete painting of Cézanne. He became a good friend of Pablo Picasso, and together they experimented with a new way of analyzing reality through painting, thereby giving rise to Cubism. Having worked closely together, the two men could not help but influence each other, and their paintings between 1910 and 1914 are very similar.

Braque also experimented with a new technique known as collage, the word *coller* in French meaning "to stick" or "to glue." The process involved combining different shapes made from pieces of newspaper, wallpaper, fabric and other materials and gluing them onto a canvas.

In the years 1929 and 1930, Braque's Cubism became less severe and less geometrical, and he painted still lifes, figures and beautifully composed landscapes. During the 1950s, he worked on the subject of birds in flight. It has been said that his final works embody all the elegance and style of French art.

PIETER BRUEGEL THE ELDER (1525/30–1569)
It is believed that Pieter Bruegel, the greatest Dutch painter of the 16th century, was born at Bruegel, near Breda, the Netherlands, sometime between 1525 and 1530. He is called the Elder to distinguish him from his son who followed closely in his footsteps.

Although Bruegel's name appears on the register of the Antwerp Guild of Painters in 1551, nothing definite is known about his early artistic training except that he was familiar with the work of Hieronymus Bosch, the great Dutch painter who was active between 1488 and 1515. It is also known that Bruegel visited Italy between 1551 and 1555, although that experience did not seem to have affected his painting. Bruegel remained firmly wedded to the Flemish tradition of realism, as well as to the portrayal of the everyday world of the common people. He produced drawings and engravings as well as paintings, capturing landscapes and scenes of daily life with a great feeling of immediacy. He is sometimes called Peasant Bruegel because so many of his pictures were inspired by country life.

CANALETTO (1697–1768)
Antonio Canal, known as Canaletto, was born and died in Venice. Although his father, a painter of stage sets, was an influence on Canaletto, a greater influence was the landscape artist Luca Carlevaris who had been in contact with northern European painters in Rome who specialized in landscapes with ancient ruins. In 1719, Canaletto also went to Rome to gain firsthand experience in this style of painting.

When Canaletto returned to Venice the following year, he began to paint *vedute* (views) of Venice for the city's many English and other foreign visitors. He painted his views on the site, complete with details, rather than later in his studio from drawings. This approach was unusual, and Canaletto later abandoned it.

Between 1741–43, Canaletto painted a series of views of Rome. Except for brief return visits to Venice, Canaletto lived in England between 1746 and 1755 painting views of London and English towns, as well as of his English clients' properties.

CARAVAGGIO (1573–1610)
Michelangelo Merisi, known as Caravaggio, was born at Caravaggio (Bergamo), Italy. He was barely twenty years old when he left Milan, where he had studied painting since childhood. His arrival in Rome, sometime between 1591 and 1593, marked a turning point in the history of European painting.

Caravaggio completed his first works, including a number of still lifes, during his early difficult days in Rome when he was an assistant in the workshops of little-known painters. It was the first time in Italy that still-life paintings had been treated as an art form. Finally, an influential patron, Cardinal del Monte, obtained an important commission for him, to paint *The Calling* and *The Martyrdom of St. Matthew* for the Contarelli Chapel in the Church of San Luigi dei Francesi. In these two powerful and highly dramatic canvases, with their strong contrasts of light and shade, Caravaggio embarked on his artistic revolution, commanding admiration as well as concern for his painting's realistic intensity which some found excessive.

In 1600–01, while still in Rome, Caravaggio painted two holy subjects, *The Martyrdom of St. Peter* and *The Conversion of St. Paul* for the Church of Santa Maria del Popolo in which he completely broke with a long iconographical tradition by portraying the two events in a down-to-earth way. People were scandalized by Caravaggio's *Madonna* for the Church of Sant' Agostino: Caravaggio pictured barefoot ne'er-do-wells kneeling in prayer to the Virgin.

In many ways, Caravaggio's paintings mirrored his own turbulent life. In 1606 he killed a man because of an unpaid gambling debt, and subsequently fled to Naples where he was able to find work. A year later, however, he had to seek sanctuary in Malta. There he again found work, although when he became involved in an argument, this time with a Knight of the Order of Jerusalem, he was thrown in jail. He succeeded in escaping to Sicily, and from there he traveled from city to city, working to pay for his return to Rome where he believed the Pope was prepared to grant him a pardon. He stopped in Naples but, hotly pursued by his old enemies, he had to flee again, this time by ship to Rome. His voyage ended tragically at Porto Ercole, where he contracted a fever that finally killed him.

Caravaggio's dramatic realism was achieved through the revolutionary technical method of painting directly onto the canvas from a model, instead of working from sketches.

VITTORE CARPACCIO (1460/65–1525/26)
Vittore Carpaccio, who was born and died in Venice, Italy, spent his life there painting large narrative series. His first series, commissioned about 1490 by the *Scuola di Sant' Orsola*, depicts scenes from St. Ursula's life; the second series, painted for the *Scuola di San Giorgio degli Schiavone* between 1502 and 1507, portrays episodes from the lives of St. George, St. Tryphon and St. James; while the third, painted for the *Scuola degli Albanesi* sometime after 1504 depicts scenes from the life of the Virgin Mary and is divided among several Italian museums. Between 1511 and 1520, Carpaccio created a series of scenes from the life of St. Stephen for the *Scuola di San Stefano*.

Carpaccio, who was primarily influenced by Gentile Bellini, combined the miniaturistic precision of the Flemish School with the grand perspective of the Italian Renaissance.

THE CARRACCI
The Carracci were a family of artists, all born in Bologna, Italy; Agostino in 1557, his brother Annibale in 1560, and their cousin, Ludovico, who introduced the two brothers to painting, in 1555. They were heirs to the Mannerist School of the late 16th century, a typically Italian style that imitated and tried to schematize the great artistic personalities of the Renaissance, sometimes with trite results. More importantly, the Carracci attempted to revive the splendors of Renaissance painting during a period of artistic uncertainty. They set up a teaching academy in Bologna, giving rise to the Bolognese School of painting, whose members included such artists as Guido Reni and Domenichino.

Annibale was the most gifted of the three, and in 1595 Cardinal Farnese invited him to Rome to decorate his family's palace. Two years later Agostino joined him, and together they painted the frescoes in the Farnese Gallery. Agostino died in 1602 before the work was finished. Annibale died in 1609, while Ludovico lived on until 1619. The work of these three men became a source of inspiration for painters of the Baroque era.

PAUL CÉZANNE (1839–1906)
Paul Cézanne was born into a wealthy family in Aix-en-Provence, France, in 1839. He attended the Collège Bourbon

there, along with the writer Émile Zola, with whom he was friends for over thirty years.

At first Cézanne's family discouraged him from becoming a painter, but in 1862 he enrolled in the Atelier Suisse in Paris and made the acquaintance of the future Impressionists. However, unhappy with life in Paris, he returned for long periods to his hometown, finally retiring to L'Estaque, near Marseilles.

Cézanne exhibited at the first Impressionist show in 1874 and again at the third one in 1877 with little success. His friend Zola used him as the model for the failed painter in his 1886 novel, *L'Oeuvre,* an incident that ended their long friendship. Cézanne, however, did enjoy a more lasting friendship with Pissarro. The latter looked upon him as a master, the two men having spent 1872 and 1873 together at Auvers-sur-Oise painting a number of works that were exhibited with the other Impressionists the following year.

After the 1877 show, Cézanne began research that led him to progress beyond Impressionism to become the "father of modern painting." Although the public was bemused by his exhibition in 1895, his first in almost twenty years, his fellow artists realized he was expressing a new concept, the idea that tone and color values must be considered as one element and not two. It is said that his work inspired Braque and Picasso in the creation of Cubism.

CIMABUE (c. 1240–1302?)

Cimabue (Cenni di Pepi) was probably born in Florence, Italy, and it was there that he first came into contact with the Byzantine painting style of Tuscany. Ironically, Cimabue himself brought Byzantine art to a close with his introduction of a new, more concrete and realistic style, which his pupil Giotto developed even further.

There are clear Byzantine influences in Cimabue's great *Crucifix* in St. Dominic's Church at Arezzo, but in his later *Crucifix* in the Church of Santa Croce in Florence, Cimabue abandoned the strict Byzantine style and achieved a more modeled quality. Cimabue's true genius manifested itself in the series of frescoes of scenes from the Gospels which he painted around 1280 in the Church of St. Francis at Assisi.

Shortly before his death, Cimabue, who also worked with mosaics, collaborated architecturally with Arnolfo di Cambio on the Florence Cathedral, where he was buried sometime after 1302.

JOHN CONSTABLE (1776–1837)

John Constable, who was one of England's greatest landscape artists, was born in East Bergholt in Suffolk, the son of a well-to-do miller. Although he originally planned to go into the religious life, he left school in 1793 to work for his father. In his spare time he studied painting with such intensity that his father allowed him to enroll as a student at the Royal Academy in London.

Because Constable's career developed slowly, he had to paint portraits to support himself. In 1811 he first successfully exhibited at the Royal Academy, his works revealing great technical mastery. In 1829 Constable was elected a full member of the Academy.

He devoted an enormous amount of work, involving hundreds of drawings and oil sketches, to the study of landscape under different atmospheric conditions and in different lights. In 1824 he exhibited three paintings at the Paris Salon and won a Gold Medal, recognition that brought him wide acclaim in France. He died in 1837 of an unknown illness.

J.-B.-CAMILLE COROT (1796–1875)

Jean-Baptiste-Camille Corot was born in Paris, began to follow his father's trade as a cloth merchant after leaving school, but soon gave up that career to paint. From the very beginning, he dedicated himself to the portrayal of landscapes in the Neoclassical manner, carefully composing his scenes and enlivening

them with historical or biblical content.

As was customary at the time, Corot executed his oil sketches outdoors, then used the sketches as a basis for the canvases which he painted in his studio. His extensive location work is documented by a large number of studies and sketches, and these have resulted in Corot being called the first "open-air" painter. Corot would never have considered the sketches to be finished works, nor would he ever have dreamed of exhibiting them. Nevertheless, today, these preparatory sketches are among his most highly prized works.

Toward the end of his life, Corot was able to absorb the ideas of new artists such as Courbet and Manet, and consequently was immensely popular with the younger generation of painters. He did much to soften the opinions of the Salons toward these controversial new artists. Although Corot enjoyed great success in his lifetime, and regularly exhibited at the official Salons, he always remained a shy, gentle and retiring person.

GUSTAVE COURBET (1819–1877)

The greatest representative of French Realist painting, Gustave Courbet, was born near the Swiss border at Ornans, in Franche-Comté, France. Although Courbet traveled to Paris in 1841 to study painting in various studios of noted artists, he actually preferred just to study the works of art in the Louvre Museum, as well as to observe nature itself. He was a very self-assured young man who soon abandoned the sentimentality of the Romantics. Nevertheless, it was not until after the events of the Revolution of 1848 that the so-called Realist movement really came to life. The popular uprising in Paris and its violent suppression had a profound effect on Courbet and other young artists of the day.

In 1850 Courbet presented his *Burial at Ornans* in the Salon and became the acknowledged head of the Realist movement and a source of inspiration for a whole new generation of painters, many of whom were later to be known as Impressionists.

A dedicated socialist, Courbet took part in the Paris Commune of 1871, assuming responsibility for what went on in the artistic sector. In this official capacity, he was held responsible for the destruction of Napoleon's column in the Place Vendôme, a symbol of the Emperor's power. In the counter-revolutionary atmosphere of post-Commune Paris, Courbet was sentenced to six months in prison for this incident and was made responsible for the cost of having the column reinstated. It was during this period that Courbet retreated into voluntary exile to Switzerland where he continued to work until his death.

LUCAS CRANACH (1472–1553)

Lucas Cranach was one of the most important German painters of the Renaissance. He was born at Kronach, Bavaria, where he remained under the guidance of his father Hans until 1498. Moving to Vienna about 1503, Cranach completed his first known paintings during this period—portraits and powerful religious works set in poetic landscapes.

The Elector of Saxony appointed Cranach court painter in 1505, which meant a move to Wittenberg, where Cranach lived for the rest of his life. Adapting his style to the taste of the Saxon court, Cranach painted severe and emotionless portraits, many of Martin Luther and other important Protestant leaders, intending them as propaganda for the new faith. Cranach painted a portrait of Titian at Augsburg in 1550, a lost masterpiece of great artistic interest.

HONORÉ DAUMIER (1808–1879)

Honoré Victorin Daumier was born in Marseilles, France, to a father who was a framer and restorer of paintings and whose ambition it was to seek his fortune in Paris. Upon arriving in Paris, however, he managed to earn only a precarious living before sending for his wife and son in 1816. The family lived in grinding poverty, and Honoré was put to work at an early age, but in his free time he studied drawing and became an apprentice to Baillard, a lithographer and printer.

In 1830 Daumier worked as a cartoonist for a new magazine, *La Caricature,* which was published until 1835 when it was suppressed. Daumier himself was sentenced to six months in prison for caricatures that openly attacked King Louis Philippe by portraying him as Gargantua. After *La Caricature* ceased publication, Daumier worked on *Charivari,* in which he satirized contemporary customs. In 1864 he left Paris and moved into a country house at Valmondois.

During the Paris Commune, Daumier became a member of the committee that was responsible for works of art in museums. His friends managed to obtain a State pension for him, and in 1878 they organized an exhibition of his works at the Durand-Ruel Gallery. Few people showed up, however, and even fewer of his works were sold.

In his four thousand lithographs, Daumier created a comprehensive portrait of 19th-century Parisian life, instilling his images with a feeling of bitter realism and a rare sense of criticism. Daumier became blind in his old age, and although Corot rescued him from total poverty, he died without ever having known real success.

JACQUES-LOUIS DAVID (1748–1825)

Jacques-Louis David, the man who was to establish Neoclassicism in France, as well as become the most important artist during the French Revolution and the Empire of Napoleon, was born into a well-to-do family in Paris.

In 1766 David entered the French Royal Academy, and in 1774 he won the Prix de Rome, which allowed him to travel to Italy to study. While in Italy, David fell under the spell of both the great Renaissance masters and the works of classical antiquity, a combination which brought about his return to classical subjects and to a simple, monumental style. David expressed his ideals in *Death of Socrates* and *Oath of the Horatii,* paintings which were exhibited in Paris. Not only were these paintings successful, but they also assured an end to the Rococo movement and established the Neoclassical style in France.

When the French Revolution broke out in 1789, David became a deputy, voting for the death of King Louis XVI. He also made himself available to the new regime, commemorating its martyrs in such paintings as *The Death of Marat.* He soon became dictator of the arts, organized and designed huge propaganda processions, and abolished the Academy, replacing it with the *Institut.*

David's career suffered a considerable setback following the fall of Robespierre in 1794, although it revived when Napoleon came to power in 1799. From then on, David devoted himself to portraying episodes from Napoleon's life, as well as creating heroic portraits of the Emperor. But when Napoleon was expelled in 1816, David too had to flee, going to Brussels as an exile. While in Brussels, where he spent the rest of his life, David returned to the subjects of his youth, painting until his death in 1825. David was also a fine teacher; his many pupils included Gérard, Girodet, Gros and Ingres.

EDGAR DEGAS (1834–1917)

Edgar Degas was born in Paris, the son of a rich banker, Auguste de Gas. Degas was introduced to painting by Henri Lamothe, a pupil of Ingres. Degas enrolled in the École des Beaux-Arts, and then made three trips to Italy (1854, 1856 and 1858), where he studied the great classics of painting.

Although Degas began by painting historical and mythological subjects, around 1865, after having met Manet and the group of artists who patronized the Café Guerbois, he gradually began painting contemporary subjects. He also became interested in the world of ballet, to which a musician friend had introduced him. This too, became a source of inspiration.

At the first Impressionist exhibition in 1874 Degas showed ten paintings. He continued to exhibit with the group until their eighth and last collective show in 1886. In some respects, however, his paintings differed from the other Impressionists since Degas did not like painting in the open air, nor was he interested in spontaneity and immediacy.

As the years passed, Degas' sight began to fail and he started to model in wax more and more. He spent his last years in isolated retirement before his death in Paris in 1917.

EUGÈNE DELACROIX (1798–1863)

Although Ferdinand Victor Eugène Delacroix was born in Charenton Saint-Maurice, France, he spent his childhood in Marseilles where his father was prefect during the First Empire. When his father died, the family moved to Paris where Eugène studied at the Lycée Impérial.

When Delacroix entered the studio of artist Baron Guérin, a follower of David's, like all apprentices, he spent time in the Louvre Museum copying the great masterpieces. In Paris Delacroix met Géricault whom he greatly admired; the two men became friends, Géricault even using Delacroix as a model for one of the shipwrecked sailors in his *Raft of the Medusa.* In 1822, Delacroix made his debut at the Salon with his painting *Dante and Virgil Crossing the Styx.* He continued to exhibit until 1859, often in direct opposition to Ingres with whom he constantly disagreed. Delacroix, who had already broken with the traditional teachings of classicism, became the best-known advocate of the Romantic movement.

When Delacroix exhibited his *Sardanapalus* at the Salon in 1827, he received only negative reactions, and, consequently, for a while, no longer received official commissions. In 1830 he supported an insurrection in Paris, more out of sentiment than any deeply felt political beliefs, and in the following year King Louis Philippe acquired his painting *Liberty Leading the People.*

Under the patronage of Adolphe Thiers, Minister of the Interior under Louis Philippe, Delacroix succeeded in obtaining important commissions for the decoration of public buildings. He was also called on to decorate the walls of the Church of Saint Sulpice.

The exhibition of forty-two of Delacroix's paintings at the Universal Exposition of 1855 was a great moment, but Delacroix's long wait for election to the Institut that same year shows how difficult it was for a noncomforming artist to be recognized over and above the deeply entrenched tradition of classicism.

For the rest of his days, Delacroix suffered from a respiratory illness that he had contracted earlier in his life, which finally resulted in his death.

DUCCIO (1255/60–1317/18)

The earliest information we have about Duccio di Buoninsegna dates from 1278, but nothing is known about his early training as an artist. Duccio was the first great painter of the Sienese School, which remained active for more than a hundred years after his death. Some historians believe that Duccio, like Giotto, was a pupil of Cimabue, and that he collaborated on the frescoes in the Church of St. Francis at Assisi.

Like Giotto, Duccio also used the Byzantine tradition as a starting point for his art, although his painting took a different path. He lightened the solemn majesty of the Byzantine figures, transforming their unearthly sanctity into a religious humanity.

Duccio's greatest work was a large altarpiece (13'4¼" × 6'11½") known as the *Maestà,* which was begun in 1308 and completed in 1311. After this date, nothing more is known about Duccio except that he probably died in 1317 or 1318.

RAOUL DUFY (1877–1953)

A study scholarship to the École des Beaux-Arts in Paris allowed Raoul Dufy to give up his classes in drawing at the night school he attended in Le Havre, France, the town where he had been born. During the early years of the 20th century, Dufy began to show his works at major collective exhibitions, with his first one-man show in 1906.

Although Dufy, who was initially attracted to the Fauves, worked in strong colors with dark outlines, he subsequently moved on to Cubism, creating severe, almost monochrome canvases. He also designed textiles, carpets and ceramics, taking part in the 1925 International Exhibit of Decorative Arts in Paris, and showing a large panel, *Electricity*, at the 1937 Universal Exposition in Paris.

After World War II, Dufy held successful one-man shows in both Paris and New York, and in 1952 he won the international prize for painting at the Venice Biennale.

ALBRECHT DÜRER (1471–1528)

Albrecht Dürer, who was a painter and engraver as well as the author of works on the theory of painting, proportion and perspective, was born in Nuremberg, Germany. His early training as an artist was influenced not only by his apprenticeship to his father, a goldsmith, but also by his numerous study tours to Italy and the Low Countries. Between 1505 and 1507, he studied the painting of Giovanni Bellini and Mantegna in Venice. Because the artistic environment of Italy had such a great influence on Dürer, he is regarded as the Northern artist most affected by the Italian Renaissance.

Between 1512 and 1519, Dürer worked mainly in Germany for Emperor Maximilian I. In 1520–21, he and his wife traveled to Flanders, where he was warmly welcomed by the artistic community. During his travels, he made many paintings and watercolors of the various cities where he stayed, as well as a number of self-portraits. Dürer became most famous for his engravings, completing his first great series, *Apocalypse*, in 1498, followed shortly after by his *Great Passion* series. Between 1513 and 1514, Dürer engraved his best-known plates: *Knight, Death and the Devil*, *St. Jerome*, and *Melancolia*. Dürer devoted the last years of his life to writing theoretical works. In addition to many portraits and religious paintings, a good number of his engravings and woodcuts have also survived.

EL GRECO (1541–1614)

El Greco, "the Greek," whose real name was Domenikos Theotokopoulos, was born in Crete where he spent his early years learning to paint icons in a style that was still essentially Byzantine. Because his family was in the service of the Venetians who controlled Crete at the time, the young painter traveled to Venice around 1560 to study Venetian painting as a pupil, it is believed, of Titian. In 1570 he traveled to Rome, where his contact with the works of the great Romano-Tuscan painters, particularly Michelangelo, was of great importance in his artistic development. Although not much is known about El Greco's activities in either Venice or Rome, all of his paintings were a product of his wide range of artistic experiences.

In 1577, El Greco was in Spain where he succeeded in obtaining a commission for the Toledo Cathedral. At the time, King Philip II was building the Escorial, a vast complex of buildings which contained a monastery, a church, the royal tombs and a retreat for himself. El Greco, who hoped to find favor with the king, painted the *Dream of Philip II*, sometimes called *Adoration of the Name of Jesus*, which was a tribute to the Christian rulers of the Holy League who had defeated the Turks at the Battle of Lepanto. Although he did, in fact, gain a commission from the king to paint *The Martyrdom of St. Maurice*, the painting failed to win royal approval.

Nevertheless, El Greco's animated compositions, with their feverish figures and eerie light effects, found favor with the Spanish nobility and the Church authorities, so much so that he received a constant stream of commissions for portraits and religious works right up until the time of his death.

PAUL GAUGUIN (1848–1903)

Paul Gauguin, who was born in Paris, began painting as a hobby, along with a colleague in the Paris stockbroker's office where they both worked. Gauguin became a student and friend of Pissarro, who introduced him to the Impressionist group. Subsequently, Gauguin exhibited at all the Impressionist shows from 1880 to 1886.

In 1883, without even telling his wife, Gauguin decided to quit his job and devote all his time to painting, a costly decision. After the breakup of the Impressionist group, Gauguin developed a highly personal style, paving the way for new experiments in painting. Van Gogh, too, was branching out on his own in the solitude of Arles, pursuing a somewhat similar direction. Although Gauguin accepted Van Gogh's invitation to join him in Arles, the two artists worked together for only a few months in 1888 when Van Gogh went tragically insane.

Meanwhile, a self-centered Gauguin, who had become intolerant of European civilization, decided to give up everything and search for a pure and primitive world. After a stay in Tahiti between 1891 and 1893, he returned to Polynesia in 1895 for good. While there, he painted a series of unique paintings in which he seemed to have reached that world he was seeking, achieving a peace of mind that had long eluded him. But in reality, they were years of great struggle for Gauguin, who had to contend with loneliness, despair and illness. He died of leprosy on May 8, 1903.

GENTILE DA FABRIANO (c. 1370–1427)

Gentile da Fabriano worked in the International Gothic style, which favored a new realism that was confined to details of animals, clothes and landscape. This International Gothic style was prevalent in France and Flanders, and by 1400 in northern Italy as well, where Gentile very possibly received his early training. Although Gentile was commissioned to paint frescoes in the Doge's Palace in Venice and commissioned to work in Brescia, none of his works from these commissions have survived.

THÉODORE GÉRICAULT (1791–1824)

Jean Louis André Théodore Géricault, who was born in Rouen, France, brought about the final break with the Neoclassical tradition, and exercised a profound influence on the works of later artists, despite his early death. Over the objections of his father, the young Géricault enrolled in the École des Beaux-Arts and rented the back of a shop in the Montmartre district of Paris to use as a studio where he had his friends pose for him. In 1814 he opened a proper studio in Montmartre close to the studios of other, more famous, artists.

In 1818 Géricault began work on what was to be his masterpiece, *The Raft of the Medusa*. Exhibited at the 1819 Salon, the painting, over which both the public and the critics were divided, failed to win a prize. By way of compensation, Géricault was invited to display the painting in London and Dublin.

Géricault next painted a highly realistic series of portraits of the mentally ill. During the same time, 1822, he worked on a series of lithographs devoted to horses. It was, in fact, two falls from horses that resulted in Géricault's suffering severe spinal damage. Although he tried to ignore the injuries, they caused him great pain, and ultimately, his death.

Géricault could be said to have founded the Romantic movement in painting, a tradition that his followers continued. However, to be a Romantic painter in France at that time was to oppose the powerful Ingres, and as a result many Romantic artists found it hard to make a living.

GIORGIONE (1476/78–1510)

Very little is known about Giorgio da Castelfranco Veneto, called Giorgione, other than that his life as an artist must have been short, perhaps no more than ten years, as he died of the plague when he was only about thirty. Giorgione, who was a pupil of Giovanni Bellini, furthered his master's research into light and color, initiating a tonal style of painting based more on the relationships and contrasts between different shades of color than on the use of chiaroscuro and perspective. His compositions also reveal an original treatment of the relationship between figures and their surroundings. Giorgione also gave a remarkable amount of space to landscape as an independent element, as can be seen in his *Tempest*.

It is believed that Giorgione was the first Venetian painter to paint small scenes for private clients using oil paints, although not a single picture is definitely documented as being his. Perhaps the most significant fact we know about Giorgione is that he greatly influenced Titian, who worked under him on a number of occasions.

GIOTTO (1266/67–1337)
According to tradition, Giotto di Bondone, who was born at Vespignano, near Florence, Italy, was introduced to painting by Cimabue. Although there is some doubt as to whether or not Giotto collaborated on the upper registers of the frescoes in the Upper Church of St. Francis at Assisi, he was definitely responsible for the layout and execution of the lower register. The lower register, which dates from the closing years of the 13th century and which his followers completed, consists of twenty-eight individual scenes depicting episodes from the life of St. Francis.

Giotto showed his full talent in his frescoes on the walls of the Scrovegni Chapel in Padua, dated about 1305, which depict the life of Mary and Jesus. He also completed two further series of frescoes around 1317 and 1325 in the Peruzzi and Bardi chapels in the Church of Santa Croce in Florence.

Giotto, who may be regarded as one of the forerunners of the Renaissance, held an important position in the history of art. He was able to absorb and develop the work done by Cimabue, achieving an even more sculptural quality in his figures, as well as making them seem more realistic and contemporary by means of facial expressions and gestures. In creating an illusion of depth, he probably referred back to the ancient mosaics whose naturalistic and architectural backgrounds displayed a rudimentary use of perspective.

FRANCISCO GOYA (1746–1828)
Francisco José de Goya y Lucientes, the greatest 18th-century Spanish painter and engraver, and one of the most important artists in Europe, was born at Fuendetodos, near Saragossa. His training was international in that José Luzan, his master at Saragossa, had studied in Naples, and Goya himself went to Rome in 1771 to study. Goya's first major commission was to paint frescoes in the Saragossa Cathedral. In 1775 he began working for the royal court, doing a series of more than fifty designs for the Royal Tapestry Works.

Goya, who was made a member of the Spanish Royal Academy in 1780, subsequently became painter to King Charles III. During this period, he painted court portraits, all in accordance with the solemnity due to the Spanish court. In 1795, during the reign of Charles IV, Goya became president of the Spanish Royal Academy, and in 1799, Principal Painter to the King.

But the weakness and political corruption of Charles IV's reign led the French Emperor Napoleon to invade Spain. Goya bitingly criticized the church and ruling class of the day in a series of engravings published under the title *Caprices*; these were soon banned from sale. Goya even managed to emphasize the coarser aspects of the royal court in his *Portrait of Charles IV and His Family*.

After the defeat of Napoleon and the "return to law," Goya painted his famous scenes of the popular Madrid insurrection on May 2, 1808, and the execution of the insurgents by firing squad on May 3. Later, he published a series of engravings entitled *Disasters of War*. The events surrounding the French invasion of Spain had a profound effect on Goya, whose style became almost Impressionistic. Goya was a great influence on later 19th-century French artists, particularly Manet.

In his portraits of the new king, Goya underlined the cruelty of the royal regime whose brutal repression affected many dissidents, including Goya himself who retired to the solitude of his house in the country, the "Quinta del Sordo" (House of the Deaf Man). A severe illness had indeed made Goya almost totally deaf. He gave artistic expression to the nightmares and visions that haunted him on the walls of his house in a series of black paintings that are as mysterious as they are vivid and disquieting.

Finally, in 1824, for his own safety, Goya retreated to the French city of Bordeaux where he continued to paint until his death in 1828.

MATHIAS GRÜNEWALD (c. 1460–1528)
Mathias Grünewald, whose real name was Mathis Gothardt, was born in Würzburg, Germany. Very little is known about his early years except that his first dated work is *The Mocking of Christ*, which he painted in 1503 for Aschaffenburg Cathedral. Grünewald became court painter to the Archbishop of Mainz in 1509.

Grünewald's greatest masterpiece is the polyptych known as the *Isenheim Altar*, which he painted for Isenheim's St. Anthony's Convent in 1515–16. The polyptych, which consists of two fixed and four movable panels painted on both sides, portrays episodes from the mystical world of St. Anthony. Grünewald did other altarpieces, but because he sympathized with the new theological ideas of Martin Luther, his relationship with the Archbishop of Mainz became strained. In 1526, the break came, and Grünewald moved, first to Frankfurt, then to Halle, where he died two years later.

Grünewald's pictures are characterized by the violent religious imagery of the High Gothic period, combined with the Italian feeling for light and color. Unlike most of his German contemporaries, Grünewald apparently never made etchings or woodcuts.

FRANCESCO GUARDI (1712–1793)
The last great Venetian artist, Francesco Guardi, was born into a family of painters in Venice and was introduced to painting in the studio of his brother, Gianantonio. Although Guardi is famous today as a painter of *vedute* (views), he started out as a figurative artist. Because most of his early works are unsigned, it is often hard to know whether they were done by Guardi or his brother Gianantonio.

As can be seen in his paintings of Venetian festivals, Guardi was undoubtedly inspired by Canaletto, although his more animated style, in which color plays an important role, is unlike Canaletto's precisely delineated perspective views. His use of color particularly owes more to his brother-in-law, Tiepolo, than to Canaletto.

Between 1760 and 1790, Guardi painted his best *vedute*, which included various episodes of Venetian public life. He was admitted very late in life to the Accademia, probably because landscape painting at that time was still regarded as a minor art form.

FRANS HALS (1581/85–1666)
In 1591, when Frans Hals was about ten years old, he and his family moved from Antwerp to Haarlem, Holland, where as a young man he attended painting school. His most brilliant portraits, which express an exuberant love of life, are those of happy, carefree young people, such as his 1624 *Laughing Cavalier* and his 1628–30 *Merry Drinker*. Nine of Hals's monumental group portraits have survived; generally they portray officials of the Haarlem Civil Guard, and in one instance a company from Amsterdam.

Although tradition portrays Hals as a drunkard and a wife-beater, there are no historical grounds for this image. It is true, however, that despite his many major commissions he was often short of money, even receiving help from the city of Haarlem toward the end of his life.

Hals continued working until late in his life. At the age of eighty-six he portrayed the *Regenten* (male governors) of the old men's almhouse, and also the *Regentessen* (female governors) of the old women's almhouse in Haarlem. These paintings are among his best works.

WILLIAM HOGARTH (1697–1764)

William Hogarth, who was born in humble circumstances in London, worked for an engraver as a young man. His first paintings, which date from between 1725 and 1728, included the series *The Harlot's Progress*, which he also turned into engravings. Works of this sort, which portrayed the virtues and vices of his day, became the mainstay of Hogarth's artistic production, and the first series was soon followed by others. Hogarth himself declared that he wanted to present exemplary moral tales "similar to representations on the stage." Because of their satirical content and pictorial inventiveness, his works enjoyed immediate and widespread success.

Although he was often the subject of savage attacks, as a writer and as an administrator of charitable institutions, Hogarth was a prominent figure in the London of his day.

HANS HOLBEIN THE YOUNGER (1497/98–1543)

Hans Holbein, who was born in Augsburg, Bavaria, into a family of painters, was called "the Younger" to distinguish him from his father, who was also an Augsburg painter. Together with his brother Ambrosius, Holbein traveled to Basle in 1515 to study in the workshop of Hans Herbster. Later he moved to Lucerne, and from there he traveled to Lombardy in 1518–19, where he studied the works of Mantegna and Leonardo, both of whom influenced his early painting.

Armed with letters of introduction from the great humanist Erasmus of Rotterdam, Holbein arrived in England in 1526, remaining there for eighteen months. While there, he was welcomed by one of King Henry VIII's ministers, Sir Thomas More; several of Holbein's famous portraits of both More and Erasmus still exist.

In 1532 Holbein returned to England, where several years later he entered the service of the royal court. The king sent Holbein to various European cities on missions, and commissioned him to paint numerous court portraits and scenes of political life. Holbein was living in London at the time of his death in 1543.

JEAN-A.-D. INGRES (1780–1867)

Jean-Auguste-Dominique Ingres was born at Montauban, France, and was introduced to music and painting by his father, who was a provincial artist versed in all aspects of art. When Ingres was eleven, he entered the Academy at Toulouse, where his teachers familiarized him with the works of Raphael, who was to have a profound influence on his art.

In 1797 Ingres traveled to Paris, where he worked in David's studio. In 1806 he went to Rome, and stayed in Italy until 1824 when he returned to Paris to exhibit at the 1825 Salon *The Vow of Louis XIII*, a painting that led Charles X to make him an officer of the Legion of Honor. From that moment on, Ingres' paintings were always hung opposite Delacroix's in the Salon, and comparison between the two became an annual event. Ingres represented the classical tradition, Delacroix represented the Romantic movement.

After a second journey to Italy in 1841, Ingres returned to Paris where he was received and entertained at Versailles by King Louis-Philippe. His commissions multiplied, particularly for portraits, and in 1855 a great retrospective exhibition of forty-three of his paintings was held at the Universal Exposition in Paris. Because the same honor was accorded to Delacroix, the rivalry continued. Unfortunately, Ingres was antagonistic to any

ideas but his own, and his high academic standing gave him t influence to oppose effectively, not only Delacroix, but also any young painter who tried to escape from a style laid down as being "correct" by Ingres. Nevertheless, Ingres continued working with great success until his death of pneumonia on January 8, 1867.

GEORGES DE LA TOUR (1593–1652)

Georges de la Tour was born at Vic, in Lorraine, France. Although little is certain about his life and works, it is known that he came from a socially ambitious family of craftsmen and farmers. It is likely that he made the almost obligatory artistic pilgrimage to Italy, and he may also have been a pupil of Guido Reni. He returned to Vic in 1617, where he married the daughter of an impoverished local nobleman who helped him gain entry into the aristocracy. In 1620 la Tour moved to Lunéville, the favorite residence of the Dukes of Lorraine, who appreciated and purchased his paintings. It was a period of prosperity for la Tour, who began to assume the airs of a country gentleman.

Meanwhile, a war was raging in Lorraine between the German emperor and the French king for control of this strategically important region which was ravaged at the time by famine and two outbreaks of the plague. After the years of hardship were over, la Tour was back in Lunéville with his family of at least ten children. He grew increasingly busy, with his studio employing both pupils and apprentices. Although his oldest son, Etienne, became involved in his father's work, when la Tour died of the plague in 1652, Etienne gave up the work and concentrated his energies on his own social advancement, finally gaining admission to the ranks of the nobility.

Georges de la Tour enjoyed great success in his lifetime, but he was subsequently almost totally ignored until the 20th century, which may explain why so little is known about him. During his lifetime, he painted religious and genre pictures which were influenced by Caravaggio; his later paintings were night scenes lit by some kind of source of light, such as a candle.

FERNAND LÉGER (1881–1955)

Born at Argentan in Normandy, France, Fernand Léger studied architecture before turning to painting in Paris where he fell under the influence of Cubism. Some critics, however, have called Léger a "tubist" rather than a Cubist, because of his fascination with machines and industry, whose geometrical shapes provided the inspiration for many of his compositions. Even his portrayal of the human figure possesses a certain mechanical quality.

Léger was also involved with theatrical design and ceramics, as well as with stained-glass window design. During World War II he lived in the United States, where the intense pace of American cities was an endless source of interest.

LEONARDO DA VINCI (1452–1519)

Leonardo, the son of Ser Pietro, a Florentine notary, was born at Vinci near Florence, Italy, on April 15, 1452. At the age of fifteen, he traveled to Florence, where he worked in the studio of Verrocchio, a talented painter and sculptor. Two works bear witness to Leonardo's early artistic maturity, *Portrait of Ginevra* and the so-called *Benois Madonna*. Two other major works, *St. Jerome* and *The Adoration of the Magi*, were still at the stage of chiaroscuro drawings when Leonardo left in 1481 for Milan, where he served Duke Ludovico Sforza, also known as Ludovico il Moro, until 1499. While in Milan, Leonardo worked on the city's canals and fortifications, planned buildings, including the dome of the cathedral, and completed such paintings as *The Virgin of the Rocks*, as well as the famous fresco, the *Last Supper*, in the refectory of the convent of Santa Maria delle Grazie.

When the French invaded Milan, Leonardo returned to Florence to work for Cesare Borgia as inspector of fortifications in Tuscany, Umbria and Romagna. He planned extraordinary feats of engineering, including a bridge over the Bosporus for Sultan Bajazet II. During this time he also worked on such masterpieces as the *Mona Lisa*, and produced a scientific paper, "Treatise on Water."

Returning to Milan, Leonardo enjoyed the protection of the French king, Louis XII, for a few years before traveling to Rome at the invitation of Giuliano de' Medici in 1513. But while in Rome, he had a difference of opinion with the Pope, so despite his advancing years, he went to Paris in response to a call from Francis I. Leonardo settled in a château at Cloux, near Amboise, where he began the task of arranging his drawings and writings. It was from these papers that his pupil Francesco Melzi assembled a collection of Leonardo's thoughts and published them after Leonardo's death under the title *A Treatise on Painting*. Leonardo was buried at Cloux, although his tomb was destroyed during the French Revolution.

EDOUARD MANET (1832–1883)

Edouard Manet was born into a wealthy and cultured Parisian family. As a student, he had a special interest in painting, and visited museums and exhibitions before finally deciding to become a painter himself. He also made numerous trips abroad to study the paintings of the past, particularly the works of the Venetian masters, as well as early 19th-century artists.

Manet became a prominent figure in the social and cultural life of Paris as well as a friend of intellectuals and writers. He exhibited at the Salon for the first time in 1861, the same year that Napoleon III, at the urging of artists whose works had been refused by the organizers of the official exhibition, allowed a showing of all rejected works in the so-called Salon des Refusés. It was there that Manet exhibited in 1863 his *Déjeuner sur l'herbe*, a painting which was bitterly criticized. Although his *Olympia*, shown at the official Salon in 1865, caused an even greater uproar, the two paintings broke the mold, allowing nonconforming artists to exhibit, thus paving the way for Impressionism. Young painters looked on Manet as the new Messiah.

In 1879 Manet fell seriously ill, although he was able to continue working until 1882. He died the following year in Paris.

ANDREA MANTEGNA (1431–1506)

Andrea Mantegna was born at Isola di Carturo, near Piazzola sul Brenta (Padua), Italy. As a child, he was entrusted by his father, who was a carpenter, to the care of Francesco Squarcione, a Paduan painter who, it is believed, adopted Mantegna as his son.

At that time, the university town of Padua, which was the greatest cultural center of northern Italy, had played host to such prominent Florentine artists as Donatello and Filippino Lippi, and Mantegna studied the works of Andrea del Castagno and Paolo Uccello in nearby Venice as well. It was against this brilliant background that Mantegna's art developed, as could be seen in his frescoes in the Ovetari Chapel in the Church of the Eremitani in Padua, almost all of which, tragically, were destroyed by bombs in World War II. Other works from this early period have survived, however, such as his polyptych in the Chapel of Santa Lucia in Padua's Church of Santa Giustina and his great altarpiece for the Church of San Zeno in Verona.

In 1453, Mantegna married Nicolosia Bellini, daughter of Jacopo and sister to Giovanni and Gentile, all three of whom were famous Venetian painters. In 1460, Ludovico Gonzaga, Duke of Mantua, hired Mantegna to work at his court, and although there are no works surviving from this date, the Bridal Chamber in the Ducal Palace was finally completed in 1474. This is Mantegna's most complex and spectacular work, which not only displayed his great talent for spatial composition, including the use of foreshortened perspective, but also his extraordinary ability as a portraitist.

Mantegna died in Mantua on September 13, 1506, and was buried in a funerary chapel he had designed in the Renaissance church of St. Andrew.

SIMONE MARTINI (c. 1284–1344)

Simone Martini, who was Duccio's pupil, was the most famous Sienese painter of the Gothic period, although his art was also influenced by developments taking place beyond the borders of Italy—particularly in France, where he lived for a number of years at the court of Robert of Anjou, the French king of Naples. The courtly world of chivalry was a constant theme in his work even when he was painting religious subjects, such as his *Maestà* in Siena's Palazzo Pubblico (Town Hall), his series of frescoes in the Lower Church of St. Francis at Assisi with its scenes from the life of St. Martin, and his famous *Annunciation* altarpiece painted for the Siena Cathedral in 1333. In 1340 Pope Benedict XII summoned Simone to Avignon, France, where he died four years later.

MASACCIO (1401–1428)

Masaccio, who was born Tomaso di Ser Giovanni di Mone in St. Giovanni Valdarno, Italy, and nicknamed Masaccio (Hulking Tom), entered the Company of St. Luke, the painters' guild, in Florence, when he was only a little more than twenty. Although he collaborated with the older and already established Masolino, he immediately displayed an independence from Masolino's late Gothic style, as well as a willingness to embrace the revolutionary new advances in Florentine art put forward in the works and ideas of Brunelleschi and Donatello.

His genius is best seen in the frescoes in the Brancacci Chapel of the Church of Santa Maria del Carmine in Florence, which depicted stories from the life of St. Peter. The frescoes display Masaccio's astonishing maturity in his treatment of the figurative ideals of the early Renaissance: the use of objective, three-dimensional space (height, width, depth), the introduction of the human figure as a tangible and central element, the realistic presentation of people and events, the decisive use of color, including dark shades, not just as a decorative element, but as a means of building up figures. Before Masaccio completed these frescoes, which are a milestone in the history of painting, he went to Rome with Masolino. There he died unexpectedly in 1428. The Brancacci Chapel was subsequently finished by Filippino Lippi in 1484. It has been said that Masaccio inherited the tradition of Giotto, and was the true ancestor of Michelangelo.

MASOLINO (c. 1383/84–1447?)

Masolino da Panicale represented Tuscan late Gothic art, which continued the 14th-century treatment of line and color, adopting certain elements of Renaissance technique without any deep sense of involvement. Masolino's great claim to fame was that he was associated with a younger painter, Masaccio, who within a few short years revolutionized Tuscan art. The two men worked together on the important frescoes in the Brancacci Chapel in the Church of Santa Maria del Carmine in Florence, a series that neither of them ever completed. Masolino outlived Masaccio, although after Masaccio's death, Masolino reverted to the more decorative style he had practiced as a young man.

Masolino worked on important commissions in Umbria and Rome and later in Lombardy, where he painted a series of frescoes for the Collegiate Church and the Baptistery at Castiglione Olona, near Como. These frescoes provide our last link with Masolino, for it is not known when or where he died.

HENRI MATISSE (1869–1954)

Henri Matisse was born at Le Château in northern France in 1869. His family, who were members of the petite bourgeoisie, wanted him to study law, but despite their opposition Matisse gave up his studies and headed for Paris to learn to paint. Of all his teachers, it was the Symbolist Gustave Moreau who recognized his talent and understood his attempts to turn painting into a product of pure color, achieved with simplicity, joy and vitality. However, Matisse had to suffer many years of poverty and humiliation before his new concept was fully understood.

It was not until 1904 that Matisse began to sell his works and hold exhibitions. Immediately, his reputation took off, and a group of artists known as the Fauves ("wild beasts") grew up around him.

While traveling through southern France, Matisse discovered the beauty of the Mediterranean landscape; it became one of his favorite subjects. He settled on the Côte d'Azur in 1921, enjoying a peaceful and productive life until the time of his death as a very old man.

MICHELANGELO BUONARROTI (1475–1564)
Because at birth Michelangelo was given over to a wet nurse whose family were stone masons in Caprese, Italy, he used to say that he had drunk in a love of sculpture with his milk. He was only thirteen when he studied in the workshop of Domenico Ghirlandaio in Florence, where he often visited the Brancacci Chapel to study Masaccio's frescoes. His first major works were sculptures, with his *Pietà*, in St. Peter's, Rome, completed in 1496.

Michelangelo's early paintings, with their clear, well-defined shapes, already displayed the monumental and sculptural characteristics of his later pictorial art. In Florence, Michelangelo's first painting commission was the *Holy Family* (1502) for Angelo Doni's wedding. The Florentine government also commissioned him to paint a fresco in the Council Hall portraying a scene from the war against the Pisans which was to be a companion piece to Leonardo's *Battle of Anghiari*. The project, which would have had the frescoes of the two greatest living artists decorating the town hall of the city where they lived, was never completed.

Michelangelo never got beyond the planning stage because he was summoned to Rome to sculpt a tomb for Pope Julius II. But when Michelangelo returned to Rome from Carrara in the winter of 1505–6, after supervising the quarrying of suitable marble for the tomb, he discovered that the Pope had changed his mind and now wanted him to paint the frescoes on the ceiling of the Sistine Chapel. Although Michelangelo constantly expressed his dislike for the project, it is now regarded as one of his greatest works of painting. As soon as he finished this enormous undertaking, he returned again to work on Pope Julius's tomb. But in 1513, the Pope died and although Michelangelo continued to work on the tomb for another three years, Julius's heirs greatly reduced the scale of the project.

When Giovanni de' Medici ascended to the papacy as Leo X, there was another change of plans, much to the annoyance of Michelangelo, who returned to Florence where he remained for the next twelve years. In Florence, the Medici family, who were at the height of their powers, entrusted Michelangelo with a number of important commissions for the monumental complex of San Lorenzo—the facade of the church, the new sacristy containing the famous tombs of Giuliano and Lorenzo, and the Laurentian Library.

Michelangelo returned to Rome when the next pope, Clement VII, asked him to decorate the altar wall of the Sistine Chapel with *The Last Judgment*, a fresco that was completed under Pope Paul III. Michelangelo, who also painted the frescoes in the Cappella Paolina, the Pauline Chapel, spent the rest of his life in Rome. He died there on February 18, 1564, at the age of ninety while working on the *Rondanini Pietà*. Michelangelo can lay claim to being the greatest sculptor, painter and draftsman who ever lived, as well as one of the world's greatest architects and poets.

CLAUDE MONET (1840–1926)
Although Claude Monet was born in Paris, he moved with his family when he was five to Le Havre, where he studied drawing. When he was eighteen, he began to concentrate on painting, and in 1859 he returned to Paris to study at the Atelier Suisse, where he met Pissarro and became a particularly avid student of the works of Delacroix.

When Monet entered the studio of Baron Gleyre, he met Re-

noir and Sisley with whom he founded an independent group of artists who were in opposition to the traditional teachings of their master. Together with other talented painters, they organized their first group exhibition in the studio of the photographer Paul Nadar in 1874. It was from Monet's painting in that exhibition, *Impression, Sunrise*, that the term "impressionism" emerged, a term that later defined the group's style.

Despite criticism, Monet remained faithful to Impressionist painting even after the group broke up. Only late in life did he earn the recognition and success he deserved.

BARTOLOMÉ ESTEBAN MURILLO (1617–1682)
In the Roman Catholic countries of 17th-century Europe, the royal courts and the Church were the two sources of commissions for artists. A painter who was not employed by a court was obliged to devote himself almost exclusively to religious subjects to ensure his success. Bartolomé Esteban Murillo was such a painter. Born in Seville, he became the most popular and famous religious painter in the Spain of his day. In addition, he achieved a considerable reputation in the rest of Europe. Although he received his early training in Seville, he developed a more mature style after he had studied and copied the masterpieces in Madrid's royal galleries.

Murillo drew inspiration from all the artistic influences to be found in Spain, developing a personal style similar to the Baroque, although lacking the Baroque's exaggeration. Even when portraying religious subjects, he never abandoned a certain feeling of realism and classical composure. Furthermore, he treated these themes with great humanity, reflecting the life and religious sentiments of the common people in his portrayal of God as well as biblical characters.

PERUGINO (c. 1450–1523)
Pietro di Cristoforo Vannucci, whose name Perugino derives from his adopted hometown of Perugia, was born in Città della Pieve, Italy. It is not definitely known if he was a pupil of Piero della Francesca at Arezzo, but it is known that he worked in Verrocchio's studio in Florence along with his contemporary, Leonardo da Vinci. Perugino's fame spread, and in 1479 he was summoned by Pope Sixtus IV to Rome, along with Botticelli and others, to paint frescoes in the apse of St. Peter's (later demolished) and on the walls of the Sistine Chapel.

After leaving Rome, Perugino again worked in Florence and Perugia, where Raphael was one of his pupils. From 1500 on, Perugino produced a great number of paintings, all with the same rather sentimentalized figures, until finally, his contemporaries grew tired of his style. He died of the plague at Fontignano, near Perugia.

PABLO PICASSO (1881–1973)
Pablo Ruiz y Picasso, who was born in Málaga, Spain, received his early artistic training from his father, a teacher at the Fine Arts Academy in Barcelona. As a young man, Picasso traveled often to Paris, where he finally settled in 1903.

In Paris, Picasso quickly distanced himself from the Fauves, whose flat shapes and bright colors were immensely popular at the time. Like Toulouse-Lautrec, Picasso chose his subjects from the world of the theater and the circus, as well as the poor, portraying them with clear outlines and occasional touches of color, either gray and blue (hence his "Blue Period") or, after 1905, pink ("Pink Period").

Between 1906 and 1910, Picasso, along with Braque, studied a new way of portraying the world on canvas, starting with simple subjects such as still lifes. Like a laboratory experiment, Picasso's canvas became a work surface on which he dismantled and reassembled objects, moving them and observing them from every angle. His style, which was no longer just a method of depicting reality, but a technique of creating forms, gave birth to Cubism.

After 1918 Picasso reverted to a more traditional style of

painting, this time on a grandiose scale, but he changed again in 1925, coming closer to the style known as Surrealism, which favored an evocative and fantastic vision of moods and events. It was during this period that he painted his great masterpiece, *Guernica.* After World War II, certain peace movements adopted Picasso's *Dove* as their symbol.

Picasso became the very personification of contemporary art, and acquired a whole flock of followers and imitators. A tireless worker, he was also involved in theatrical design and book illustration, as well as painting many portraits of famous writers and musicians. His fame spread, and today his works are shown in countless museums around the world.

Picasso's death in 1973 at Mougins, France, after a long and brilliant life, marked the end of an artistic era.

PIERO DELLA FRANCESCA (1410/20–1492)
Piero della Francesca, who was born and died at Sansepolcro in Umbria, Italy, received his early training in Florence during the first third of the 15th century. In 1442, Piero was back in San Sepolcro to work on an altarpiece, *Madonna della Misericordia* (Our Lady of Mercy), which he finished sometime later. In 1449–50, Piero worked at Ferrara and Rimini, and in 1452, he began work on the great series of frescoes depicting the story of the True Cross, in the Church of St. Francis at Arezzo. He traveled often to Urbino, where he painted the double portrait of Duke Federico da Montefeltro and his wife Battista Sforza, and other important works such as *Madonna with Duke Federico da Montefeltro as Donor.*

Piero, whose most famous pupils were Perugino and Signorelli, made an important contribution toward the scientific definition of perspective. Near the end of his life, when it is believed he was blind, he devoted his time to writing two treatises on perspective and geometry. Piero arranged his figures perfectly within their settings and portrayed their beautiful contemporary costumes with an extraordinary attention to detail. Although his figures have a sculptural sense of solidity, they also express such a strong sense of self-absorption, they sometimes seem remote.

CAMILLE PISSARRO (1831–1903)
Camille Pissarro, who was born in St. Thomas in the French Antilles, West Indies, was sent by his parents to study in Paris, first at the École des Beaux-Arts, then at the Atelier Suisse, where he met Monet and Cézanne. His parents reluctantly gave him permission to become a painter after he had run off to Venezuela with a Danish artist.

Pissarro's artistic development was greatly influenced by his contacts with Corot, and to an even greater extent with Courbet, who introduced him to the Realist group of artists. In 1865–66 he became friendly with the artists of the Café Guerbois and participated in all the Impressionist exhibitions. He was the oldest member of the group, becoming a mentor for the younger artists—Cézanne, Gauguin and Van Gogh.

Although Pissarro's works had been well accepted at the official Salons between 1860 and 1870, after joining the Impressionist group he no longer wanted to exhibit at the Salon. Out of loyalty to his friends, he shared their difficulties, even though he had a wife and six children to support. Although he suffered from a serious eye problem, he was a prolific worker. At the time of his death, Pissarro was completely blind.

RAPHAEL (1483–1520)
Raphael, whose real name was Raffaello Sanzio, was born in Urbino, Italy, the son of the painter Giovanni Santi, who died when Raphael was only eleven. Dominated by the elegant court of the Dukes of Montefeltro, the cultural and artistic environment of Urbino was an enormous influence on Raphael's development as an artist. Urbino, which was the birthplace of the architect Bramante, was full of architectural masterpieces, as well as works by the artist Piero della Francesca. Raphael's de-

velopment was also influenced by the Umbrian School of painting represented by Perugino, who is believed to have been Raphael's master.

Raphael's style reached its full maturity when he settled in Florence in 1506. There he derived inspiration for his own unique and highly personal style by studying and assimilating the great works of the Tuscan Quattrocento (15th century), as well as Flemish painting and the art of Leonardo.

In 1508, Pope Julius II summoned Raphael to Rome to decorate the *Stanze* (rooms) of his new residence in the Vatican. Raphael tackled subjects of great complexity in these rooms, succeeding in uniting them in a series of carefully balanced and majestic compositions. He also supervised the building of St. Peter's, altering the original centralized layout designed by Bramante by lengthening its basic shape. While in Rome, he also completed a famous series of portraits—among them *Leo X* and *Baldassare Castiglione*—as well as a number of equally famous Madonnas, including the *Madonna della Sedia* (Madonna of the Chair).

Raphael, who was one of the most famous painters of the High Renaissance, died suddenly on April 6, 1520, while still working on his last great work, *The Transfiguration.*

REMBRANDT VAN RIJN (1606–1669)
Another giant of 17th-century painting was Rembrandt van Rijn, although he differed radically both temperamentally and artistically from Rubens. Rembrandt, who was born in Leyden, Holland, the son of a miller, received his training first in Leyden, then in Amsterdam. His master, Pieter Lastman, had lived in Italy and had acquired certain figurative and technical traits from Mannerism and Renaissance Classicism. Rembrandt, however, always retained his links with the Flemish tradition of realism which was a distinctive feature of his art.

In the newly independent Protestant provinces of the Netherlands, there were no kings to work for, and no richly decorated churches to embellish either. Instead, commissions came from rich traders and merchants, guilds and trade associations, private citizens and companies of civil guards. For the Surgeons' Guild in Amsterdam, Rembrandt painted *The Anatomy Lesson of Dr. Tulp* and *The Anatomy Lesson of Dr. Deyman.* For the Drapers' Guild, he painted a portrait of the Guild's magistrates, while for the company of Captain Frans Banning Cocq, he painted the so-called *Night Watch*, not only his most famous painting, but also one of the best-known paintings of all time.

In later life, Rembrandt's long series of portraits were restricted to ones of his friends and family. In contrast to his realistic style, which was based on the strong use of chiaroscuro, people gradually began to prefer the lighter and more refined style of other painters, and as a result Rembrandt's last masterpiece, *The Conspiracy of the Batavians*, which was commissioned by the City Council for Amsterdam's new Town Hall, was rejected outright. Today, only the central section of this painting survives, hanging in Stockholm's National Museum. In his later years, Rembrandt also turned to biblical subjects, establishing a Protestant view of religion in his paintings.

Rembrandt, who died in poverty in 1669, was not only a painter, but also an excellent engraver, and a whole series of self-portraits, both prints and paintings, have survived. These self-portraits clearly illustrate the various stages in Rembrandt's often difficult life.

AUGUSTE RENOIR (1841–1919)
The son of a tailor of modest means, Pierre Auguste Renoir was born at Limoges, France. He moved to Paris with his family when he was four, and at fourteen enrolled in a night school to learn drawing, while working by day first in a china factory and later as a fabric designer.

In 1862 Renoir entered the École des Beaux-Arts, meeting

Monet, Sisley and Pissarro in Baron Gleyre's studio. With them, along with Degas, Cézanne and the photographer Paul Nadar, Renoir attended meetings at the Café Guerbois where the artists collaborated on organizing the original Impressionist exhibition.

Renoir was one of the first Impressionists to be accepted by the public, perhaps because his paintings had such a gentle feeling. During a trip to Italy in 1881, he was greatly taken by the paintings of Raphael and the frescoes of Pompeii, and upon returning to Paris he rediscovered Ingres. These experiences helped him to introduce a greater feeling of body and volume into his paintings.

Although he was crippled with arthritis and had to tie the brush onto his hand, Renoir continued painting until he was very old. During his last years he saw a good deal of Matisse, whom he greatly admired.

SIR JOSHUA REYNOLDS (1723–1792)

Some critics regard Sir Joshua Reynolds as the most important figure in the history of English painting. Born at Plympton St. Maurice in Devon, and educated in the classical disciplines, Reynolds began his art studies under Thomas Hudson in London in 1740. In 1749, he traveled to Rome for two years, an experience that had a lifelong influence on him.

After his return to London, he began to enjoy widespread success as a portrait painter. In 1760, the Incorporated Society of Artists was founded in London, and the first public exhibitions of contemporary paintings were held. In 1768, under the patronage of George III, the Royal Academy was established, with Reynolds as its president, a position he filled with great success. His *Discourses*, first delivered as lectures at the Royal Academy, was a kind of guide for young artists.

From 1769 on, the Academy showed all of Reynolds' best works. His range included both historical paintings and portraits, particularly lively and affectionate renditions of children. Reynolds, who painted every British man and woman of importance in the second half of the 18th century, was struck down by paralysis in 1772. In the years following, his eyes failed gradually. He died in 1792.

ROGIER VAN DER WEYDEN (c. 1400–1464)

Rogier van der Weyden, who was born at Tournai in southern Flanders, was probably also the artist known as Rogier de la Pasture who entered the Tournai Guild of Painters in 1432 after serving an apprenticeship to Robert Campin. Although it is fairly easy to trace Rogier's later works, a series of religious paintings now scattered throughout the major museums and galleries of the world, Rogier didn't sign or date his early paintings, and art historians have attributed many of them to Robert Campin.

Rogier enjoyed the patronage of the Dukes of Burgundy, and while in Italy, he attended the courts of the Este family in Ferrara, as well as the Medici in Florence. Although the inspiration for certain elements of his composition were probably derived from his knowledge of Italian art, he retained a Gothic style based on strongly defined and rhythmical outlines. While his clarity of color and his underlying sense of realism were inspired by van Eyck and the Flemish tradition, Rogier approached his subjects with more warmth and emotion.

PETER PAUL RUBENS (1577–1640)

Peter Paul Rubens, the most important artist of his day in northern Europe, and considered by many to be the greatest Flemish painter of all time, was born in Siegen, Germany, where his father had been forced to emigrate because of his Calvinist beliefs. Ten years later, however, his widowed mother took Rubens back to Antwerp, Belgium, which was still under the control of Catholic Spain. Rubens was later to become an important figure in the Catholic courts of Europe.

In 1600, Rubens arrived in Italy, where his artistic talents developed. He painted a number of important works in Mantua, and in Genoa he produced a successful series of portraits of nobles and merchants. Upon hearing that his mother was dying, Rubens returned to Antwerp in 1608. It was there that he later built a large Italian palace and embarked on perhaps the most energetic and fruitful career in the history of art.

Rubens' style of painting is vigorous, vital, and exuberant, a classic example of Baroque art. After completing the *Raising of the Cross* and the *Descent from the Cross*, works of great dramatic intensity which he created for Antwerp Cathedral, Rubens, in 1622, began a series of twenty-one paintings on the life of Marie de' Medici, Queen of France.

Rubens remained prolific as a painter while still doing a good deal of traveling on various diplomatic missions. In 1628 he was sent to Madrid on a mission to Philip IV; during this time he met Velazquez and also completed forty paintings, including a portrait of the King and royal family. In 1629 he spent nine months in London, where he was knighted by Charles I.

One of the reasons Rubens was able to produce such a staggering number of paintings was that he ran an efficient studio where he carried out the groundwork on paintings that his highly skilled assistants later finished.

GEORGES SEURAT (1859–1891)

Born in Paris, Georges Seurat entered the French Academy in 1879. Interested in the Impressionists' theories on light and color, he hoped to learn a set of general rules from them that would enable him to create a more scientific approach to painting. After many experiments made in conjunction with his friend Paul Signac, he invented a technique of applying small dots, or points, of color—yellow, blue, red—to the canvas in order to achieve variations of shade without losing any of the color's brilliance.

Seurat gained the backing of Pissarro and was allowed to show some of his works at one of the Impressionists' exhibitions. His new style of painting was favorably received by some of the critics, who called it Post-Impressionism, or Divisionism, although today it is known as Pointillism.

ALFRED SISLEY (1839–1899)

Of English descent, Alfred Sisley was born in Paris and attended school there before being sent to an English university by his parents. When he returned to Paris in 1862, Sisley, who had already shown an interest in painting, became a full-time artist and a pupil of Baron Gleyre. Along with Monet and Renoir, he began to experiment with open-air Impressionist painting. He also exhibited in the official Salons of 1866, 1868 and 1870.

The Franco-Prussian War of 1870 ruined Sisley's family financially, and Sisley too found himself in serious financial straits. Although a one-man show was organized for him at the Durand-Ruel Gallery in 1883, he never enjoyed real success, and his lack of money often forced him to swallow his pride and write to friends begging them to buy one of his paintings for a nominal amount. Consequently, after his death in 1899 at Moret-sur-Loire, it was his friends, and not he, who made money from his work.

GIAMBATTISTA TIEPOLO (1696–1770)

After the lean artistic years of the Baroque period which actually never touched Venice, the artistic genius of Giambattista Tiepolo emerged in that city. Although he studied under a relatively minor artist, Gregorio Lazzarini, Tiepolo soon found himself attracted to the more animated and dramatic compositions of other Venetian painters such as Giovanni Piazzetta and Paolo Veronese. He finally developed his own style, combining the grandeur of Baroque composition with the colorism of Venetian Renaissance painting.

In 1751 Tiepolo was invited to Würzburg, Germany, to decorate the residence of the Prince-Bishop of Franconia. Tiepolo's last major undertaking was in Spain, where he arrived in 1762 at the invitation of King Charles III to paint frescoes in the Hall of the Ambassadors in the Royal Palace of Madrid. But Tiepolo's genius was not fully appreciated in Spain. After his death there in 1770, seven canvases he had done for the Church of San Pasqual at Aranjuez were taken down. Nevertheless, Tiepolo had a great influence on Spanish art, particularly on Goya, who held him in high regard.

Certainly Tiepolo enjoyed an extremely successful career over the years and was the most representative Venetian painter of the 18th century. He left superb examples of his work in the palaces of Venice and the villas of the Veneto (the region surrounding Venice), as well as in Lombardy where he worked between 1730 and 1740. Nevertheless, for all his genius, he was an example of a great artist confined by an artistic tradition that was in decline.

TINTORETTO (1518–1594)
Jacopo Robusti, born in Venice, was better known as Tintoretto, his nickname acquired as a result of his father's trade as a dyer, or *tintore*. According to tradition, Tintoretto was an apprentice in Titian's workshop, but was thrown out because of his method of working, as well as for his preference for Michelangelo and the Roman Mannerist painters.

Tintoretto's first masterpieces were *The Last Supper*, which he painted for the Church of San Marcuola in Venice in 1547, and *St. Mark Rescuing a Slave*, which dates from 1548. Venice's Church of San Rocco awarded Tintoretto a major commission in 1549, establishing his reputation as a painter. The following year, he married the daughter of a Venetian banker. The Venetian nobility, the Church and Venice's *scuole*, or guilds, all commissioned Tintoretto with a constant flow of work, and in 1564, he began a lifelong association with the Scuola di San Rocco which was instrumental in turning the guild into one of Venice's greatest attractions.

During the same period, Tintoretto completed his decoration in the Scuola di San Marco and worked on his gigantic canvases for the Doges' Palace (these were completed after his death in 1594).

Tintoretto, who left a flourishing studio in the hands of his sons Domenico and Marco, expressed in his will a desire to be buried in the Church of Santa Maria dell' Orto.

TITIAN (1490–1576)
The tonal painting of Giorgione was developed further by his contemporary, Tiziano Vecelli, known as Titian. Born at Pieve di Cadore, Italy, Titian was sent to nearby Venice at an early age to learn to paint, first under the Bellini, then under Giorgione. After their deaths, Titian, who had carefully studied the lessons these great masters of Venetian painting had to teach, became established quickly in his own right. On the death of Giovanni Bellini in 1516, Titian became Painter to the Republic of Venice.

In 1516, Titian was commissioned to paint an altarpiece depicting *The Assumption* for the Church of Santa Maria dei Frari, which amazed both the Venetian people and the Franciscan friars with its liveliness and daring composition. Titian achieved extraordinary fame with his subsequent works. From Ferrara, Alfonso d'Este commissioned three mythological paintings, although from letters it is known that work on them was interrupted several times because of Titian's other commitments. Titian then devoted a good deal of time to portraits, including one of Charles V, which so pleased the Emperor that he made Titian a Palatine Count.

When Titian was in Rome in 1545–46, he came in contact with the great works of the famous 16th-century Romano-Tuscan painters without ever compromising his own artistic identity. During his time in Rome, he painted his famous and revealing portrait *Pope Paul III and His Grandsons*, which, rather than a work of slavish adulation, had a distinctly critical

quality. Because Charles V's son, Philip II of Spain, continued to request paintings with mythological subjects, Titian returned to the compositions of his youth, exploiting the effects of color to a much greater extent than he once had. In his last works, this colorist style became enriched by blazes of light that endowed his figures with an even more vibrant and expressive quality.

Titian died on August 17, 1576, comforted by his sons Orazio and Pomponio, painters of modest talent whom their father had tried in vain to introduce into the courts of Europe. Titian was certainly the greatest of all Venetian painters, and is also considered by some to be the founder of modern painting.

HENRI DE TOULOUSE-LAUTREC (1864–1901)
Henri Marie Raymond de Toulouse-Lautrec was born at Albi, the son of provincial French aristocrats. Although he showed a talent for drawing as a child, he did not become really involved until he was confined to bed after breaking his legs in two accidents, in 1878 and 1879, which left him permanently deformed.

After his parents gave Henri permission to paint full-time, his mother outfitted her Parisian flat for him. While in Paris, Toulouse-Lautrec visited the studios of the best-known artists of the day. He met Van Gogh in 1886.

In 1884 Toulouse-Lautrec rented a studio in Montmartre, the bohemian district of Paris filled with cafés and theaters. Toulouse-Lautrec made Montmartre his world, not just as an observer, but as an eager participant in its enthusiastic night life. Because drawing allowed him to capture a precise moment in time by means of a series of rapidly executed lines, he preferred drawing to painting.

Although the hectic and dissipated life Toulouse-Lautrec led in Montmartre seemed to invigorate him at first, it eventually resulted in his collapse. In 1899 he tried to cure himself of alcoholism in a clinic at Neuilly. After his return to Paris, apparently fully recovered, he suffered a paralysis in 1901. He retreated to his mother's house in the country, where he died in September of that year.

JOSEPH M.W. TURNER (1775–1851)
Joseph Mallord William Turner was born into a poor London family, but success came early. From his youth, Turner displayed a passion for drawing and watercolor painting, and at the age of fourteen he was admitted to the Royal Academy.

Turner's main interest was landscape art, and as early as 1793 he was awarded a prize by the Society of Artists for a landscape drawing. In 1794 he exhibited a series of watercolors at the Academy, and two years later his first oil painting was shown there. In 1799 Turner was elected an associate member of the Royal Academy; in 1802 he became a full member and in 1807 he was appointed Professor of Perspective. During this period Turner traveled throughout England, creating numerous albums of sketches and studies of the English countryside.

The landscapes from the early decades of Turner's career display a sense of classical composition and often portray historical or mythological scenes. Around 1827–28, Turner's style of painting changed, revealing a more personal quality which ran the risk of alienating his patrons. Even with his new and looser technique—in which color flowed freely and seemingly independent of the basic design—Turner's paintings remained essentially Romantic. Nature, which is never simply observed, stood revealed as a powerful source of emotion.

Turner, who was buried in St. Paul's Cathedral, left in his will 300 paintings and 20,000 watercolors and drawings to England. At present, there are plans for these works to be housed in a special gallery in Somerset House in London.

PAOLO UCCELLO (1397–1475)
Paolo di Dono, better known as Paolo Uccello, was born in Florence, Italy, where his early training as a painter and mosaicist was based on the new theories of the early Renaissance. At the age of twenty-eight, Uccello moved to Venice and it was there that he came into contact with the late Gothic

tradition of northern Italy. Uccello also worked at Padua, where he may have influenced the painter Mantegna, as well as at Urbino, where the surviving section of his *predella* with its scenes of *The Miracle of the Profaned Host* are of particular importance because of his use of perspective. Uccello's best-known works are the three panels of *The Battle of San Romano*, which have since been split up among various museums.

ANTHONY VAN DYCK (1599–1641)

Anthony van Dyck, who was born in Antwerp, the son of a wealthy silk merchant, was sent as an apprentice at the age of ten to the studio of Hendrik van Balen, a successful Antwerp painter. An even greater influence on van Dyck than van Balen, however, was Rubens, for whom van Dyck worked as an assistant while still in his teens. Rubens had recently returned from Italy, and was well on his way to becoming the leading figure in Flemish painting. In 1618, van Dyck was enrolled in the Antwerp Guild of Painters, probably collaborating with Rubens on various works.

In 1620, van Dyck made his first trip to England. There he was offered a permanent position at the court of James I. He declined the offer, however, since he had his heart set on a planned trip to Italy. The year 1627 saw van Dyck back in Antwerp. Because Rubens was off on a diplomatic mission at the time, all the most important commissions were given to van Dyck.

In 1632 van Dyck returned to England where he enjoyed enormous success, with Charles I appointing him court painter as well as knighting him. Van Dyck organized a huge studio; his subjects sat for him only by appointment. Before long, he was richer than his aristocratic clients.

However, fearing the imminent downfall of the British monarchy, van Dyck returned to Antwerp in 1640, the year Rubens died. In 1641, van Dyck traveled to Paris but, failing to obtain commissions there, returned to England. Tired and ill, he died in 1641 and was buried according to his wishes, in St. Paul's Cathedral in London. He was only forty-two years old, but had produced a vast body of work, the most consistent type being his portraits, which had a lasting influence on such later great English portraitists as Reynolds, Gainsborough and Lawrence.

JAN VAN EYCK (c. 1385–1441)

Jan van Eyck was probably the younger brother of Huybrecht, with whom it is believed he collaborated on the large and influential altarpiece of St. Bavon in Ghent. Although a good deal is known about Jan, the activities and even the existence of his older brother are the subject of a good deal of controversy. Nevertheless, the van Eyck paintings represent the full flowering of Flemish art.

Jan became a court painter to Count John of Holland about 1422, with a commission to decorate his palace at The Hague. After the Count's death, Jan worked for Philip the Good, Duke of Burgundy, whom he served for the rest of his life. The Duke assigned many diplomatic missions to Jan, who used his travel experiences to introduce an element of mystery into the background landscapes of his paintings.

Although his style reflected an unemotional attitude that amounted to coldness, it was Jan's portraits which brought him his greatest fame. They were characterized by a carefully studied use of shading and an extraordinary talent for perfectly reproducing the smallest details.

VINCENT VAN GOGH (1853–1890)

Vincent Van Gogh was born in Groot-Zundert, Holland, to a Protestant clergyman father who encouraged him to become an art dealer like his brother Theo. Vincent loved painting, but he was no good as a businessman, and in 1876 he gave up his job without knowing what he wanted to do. He tried several jobs in different cities, studied drawing in Brussels, then enrolled in the Academy at Antwerp. He soon gave this up, too, and went to Paris to join his brother.

Theo, who was working at the Goupil Gallery, put Vincent in touch with the Impressionists and Vincent met Toulouse-Lautrec and became friendly with Gauguin. The two years he spent in Paris, 1886–1888, were important in the development of his art. Van Gogh, restless, and anxious not to be a burden to his now-married brother, left Paris for Arles in the south of France, where he lived a solitary life. In the bright Mediterranean light of Arles, he developed a highly personal style that went beyond the boundaries of Impressionism.

When people began to define Van Gogh's style, they spoke for the first time of Expressionism, meaning a method of painting that is not bound up with visual reality, but which tries to communicate the innermost feelings of the artist.

Gauguin was the only friend who came to visit Van Gogh at Arles, staying there for two months. But there was an inevitable clash of personalities, and one day, exasperated by continual quarrels and arguments, Van Gogh attacked his friend with a razor, afterward punishing himself by cutting off his own ear. It was the first sign of madness that was to haunt him for the rest of his life.

Van Gogh had to be admitted to an insane asylum for some months, after which he returned to Paris, where a friend of Pissarro's, Dr. Gachet, looked after him. Although he seemed to be recovering, after a few months he again became deeply depressed and in desperation shot himself on July 29, 1890.

VELAZQUEZ (1599–1660)

Spain's most famous painter, Diego Rodriguez de Silva y Velazquez, who was born in Seville, entered the workshop of the painter Francisco Pacheco at the age of ten. In 1618 Velazquez married Pacheco's daughter Juana. Pachecho helped Velazquez gain entry into the Spanish court and in 1623 the latter was appointed court painter, completing his first portrait of Philip IV the same year. His career at court was slow, although during that period he painted portraits of the court's principal figures, such as Count-Duke Olivares, the powerful prime minister.

Although Velazquez met Rubens in 1628 in Madrid, he remained relatively unaffected by Rubens' Baroque style. A year later, Velazquez obtained permission from the king to travel to Italy. He stayed for more than a year, visiting the major cities.

Velazquez traveled to Italy a second time twenty years later in order to acquire works of art for the Royal Gallery. The king requested several times that he come back to Spain, but Velazquez continually postponed his return. While in Rome, Velazquez managed to obtain permission to paint a portrait of Pope Innocent X which became famous for its harmonious use of different shades of red.

Velazquez's paintings of members of the Spanish royal family in hunting costumes, with gentle, misty landscapes in the background are particularly fine. His last great work, and perhaps his best-known painting, was *Las Meninas*, which contains a self-portrait.

JAN VERMEER (1632–1675)

Very little is known about the life and works of the great Dutch painter Jan Vermeer. His surname, a contraction of Van der Meer ("from the sea"), was shared by several painters of the time and has resulted in confusion. All we know for certain is that Jan Vermeer was christened in Delft, Holland, on October 31, 1632, was married in April of 1652 and was buried in Delft on December 5, 1675. It is also known that he was admitted to the Guild of Painters in December of 1652, acting as its president in 1670–71.

Although the only key to understanding his life lies in his paintings, these too, are surrounded with mystery, having been completely forgotten until the 19th century. Only thirty-five paintings have definitely been attributed to Vermeer, which is perhaps why it has been suggested that his main occupation was that of an art dealer.

155

ILLUSTRATIONS

The dimensions (width × height) of each work are given in both centimeters and inches, together with the date of the work and its present location.

61 Albrecht Dürer
Feast of the Rose Garlands
194.5 × 162 cm. (76⅗" × 63⅘"), 1506
Prague, National Museum

61 Albrecht Dürer
Rhinoceros
21.2 × 30 cm. (8⅓" × 11⅘"), 1515

63 Albrecht Dürer
Noli me tangere
(from the *Little Passion* series of woodcuts)
12.7 × 9.7 cm. (5" × 3⅘"), 1510

64 Mathias Grünewald
St. Anthony and St. Paul
(part of the *Isenheim Altar*)
141 × 265 cm. (55⅗" × 104⅖"), 1512–16
Colmar, Unterlinden Museum

64 Mathias Grünewald
Temptation of St. Anthony
(part of the *Isenheim Altar*)
139 × 265 cm. (54¾" × 104⅖"), 1512–16
Colmar, Underlinden Museum

65 Albrecht Altdorfer
Susannah
61.2 × 74.8 cm. (24⅕" × 29½"), 1526
Munich, Alte Pinakothek

66 Lucas Cranach the Elder
Venus and Cupid
67 × 169 cm. (26⅖" × 66⅗"), 1531(?)
Rome, Borghese Gallery

67 Lucas Cranach the Elder
Crucifixion
99 × 138 cm. (39" × 54⅖"), 1503
Munich, Alte Pinakothek

68 Hans Holbein the Younger
Henry VIII
75 × 88.2 cm. (29⅗" × 34¾"), 1539–40
Rome, National Gallery

70 Michelangelo
Sketches for the Medici tombs in Florence
London, British Museum

72 Michelangelo
The Last Judgment
1120 × 1370 cm. (441¼" × 145¾"), 1537–41
Rome, Vatican Palace, Sistine Chapel

74 Giorgione
The Castelfranco Madonna
152 × 200 cm. (60" × 78⅘"), c. 1504
Castelfranco Veneto, Church of San Liberale

75 Titian
Pope Paul III with his Grandsons
174 × 210 cm. (68⅗" × 82¾"), 1546
Naples, Capodimonte Museum

77 Tintoretto
Battle Between Pirates
307 × 186 cm. (121" × 73¼"), c. 1580
Madrid, Prado Museum

78 El Greco
The Dream of Philip II
110 × 140 cm. (43⅓" × 55⅕"), 1579
Madrid, Escorial

79 El Greco
Pentecost
127 × 275 cm. (50" × 108⅓"), 1605–10
Madrid, Prado Museum

81 Pieter Bruegel the Elder
Flemish Proverbs
163 × 117 cm. (64¼" × 46"), 1559
Berlin, Straatliche Museen

83 Caravaggio
The Conversion of St. Paul
175 × 230 cm. (69" × 90⅗"), 1600–01
Rome, Church of Santa Maria del Popolo

83 Caravaggio
The Martyrdom of St. Peter
175 × 230 cm. (69" × 90⅗"), 1600–01
Rome, Church of Santa Maria del Popolo

85 Peter Paul Rubens
The Descent of the Cross
(central panel of triptych)
312 × 421 cm. (123" × 165⅞"), 1612
The Visitation; The Presentation in the Temple
(side panels of triptych)
150 × 420 cm. (59" × 165½"), 1614
Antwerp Cathedral

87 Peter Paul Rubens
The Marriage by Proxy in Florence
(from the series *The Life of Marie de' Medici*)
295 × 394 cm. (116¼" × 155¼"), 1622–25
Paris, Louvre Museum

88 Rembrandt van Rijn
The Anatomy Lesson of Dr. Tulp
216.5 × 169.5 cm. (85⅓" × 66¾"), 1632
The Hague, Mauritshuis

91 Rembrandt van Rijn
The Night Watch
438 × 359 cm. (172⅗" × 128⅞"), 1642
Amsterdam, Rijksmuseum

92 Anthony van Dyck
Portrait of Cardinal Guido Bentivoglio
145 × 196 cm. (57⅛" × 77¼"), 1623
Florence, Pitti Palace

93 Anthony van Dyck
King Charles I
212 × 272 cm. (83½" × 107⅕"), 1635
Paris, Louvre Museum

94 Diego Velazquez
Philip IV
314 × 301 cm. (123⅔" × 118⅗"), 1635
Madrid, Prado Museum

95 Diego Velazquez
Philip IV
102 × 201 cm. (40⅕" × 79⅕"), 1628
Madrid, Prado Museum

97 Frans Hals
Portrait of W. van Heythusen
37.5 × 46.5 cm. (14¾" × 18⅓"), 1637–39
Brussels, Musées Royaux des Beaux-Arts de Belgique

98 Jan Vermeer
The Milkmaid
41 × 45.5 cm. (16⅛" × 18"), 1658–60
Amsterdam, Rijksmuseum

98 Jan Vermeer
The Love Letter
30.5 × 44 cm. (12" × 17⅓"), 1667
Amsterdam, Rijksmuseum

98 Jan Vermeer
Girl Reading by a Window
64.5 × 83 cm. (25⅖" × 32¾"), 1657
Dresden, Art Gallery

100 Georges de la Tour
Virgin and Child
91 × 76 cm. (35⅞" × 30"),?
Rennes, Musée des Beaux-Arts

101 Annibale Carracci
Polyphemus Attacking Acis and Galatea
1597–1604
Rome, Farnese Palace

103 Bartolomé Esteban Murillo
Madonna and Child
105 × 155 cm. (41⅖" × 61"), c. 1650–60
Florence, Pitti Palace

105 Sir Joshua Reynolds
Master Hare
63.5 × 77 cm. (25" × 30⅓"), 1788–89
Paris, Louvre Museum

106 John Constable
The Water-Mill at Gillingham in Dorset
52 × 63 cm. (20½" × 24⅘"), 1827
London, Victoria and Albert Museum

106 John Constable
The Valley of the Stour
77.8 × 55.5 cm. (30⅔" × 21⅞"), ?
Boston, Museum of Fine Arts

106 John Constable
Boat Building near Flatford Mill
61.6 × 51 cm. (24¼" × 20"), 1815
London, Victoria and Albert Museum

107 William Hogarth
The Ball
90 × 68.5 cm. (35½" × 27"), 1745
London, South London Art Gallery

107 William Hogarth
The "Indian Emperor"
146.5 × 131 cm. (57½" × 51⅗"), 1731–32
Galway Collection

109 Giambattista Tiepolo
The Investiture of Bishop Harold
1752
Würzburg, Residenz

110 Francesco Guardi
Concert for the Counts of the North
90 × 67 cm. (35½" × 26⅖"), 1782
Munich, Alte Pinakothek

110 Francesco Guardi
The Doge at the Church of the Salute
100 × 68 cm. (39" × 26⅘"), 1770–75(?)
Paris, Louvre Museum

113 Canaletto
The Grand Canal and the Bembo Palace
80 × 47 cm. (31½" × 18½"), 1730–31
Woburn Abbey, Duke of Bedford Collection

114 Francisco Goya
The Third of May, 1808
345 × 266 cm. (134" × 104⅘"), 1814
Madrid, Prado Museum

116 Jacques-Louis David
Napoleon Crossing the Alps
259 × 221 cm. (102" × 87"), 1800–01
Château de la Malmaison

118 J.-B.-Camille Corot
Castelgandolfo
(detail from *Souvenirs d'Italie*)
81 × 65 cm. (32" × 25⅗"), 1865
Paris, Louvre Museum

119 Joseph M.W. Turner
Crossing the Brook
165 × 193 cm,. (65" × 76"), 1815
London, National Gallery

120 Jean-A.-D. Ingres
La Grande Odalisque
162 × 91 cm. (63⅞" × 35⅞"), 1814
Paris, Louvre Museum

121 Jean-A.-D. Ingres
Marie-Françoise Beauregard Rivière
70 × 100 cm. (27⅗" × 39"), 1805
Paris, Louvre Museum

122 Gustave Courbet
Burial at Ornans
663 × 314 cm. (261¼" × 123¾"), 1849
Paris, Louvre Museum

123 Théodore Géricault
Raft of the Medusa
716 × 491 cm. (300" × 193½"), 1818–19
Paris, Louvre Museum

124 Honoré Daumier
Theatrical Scene with Two Comedians
82 × 60.5 cm. (32⅓" × 23⅘"), 1864
Paris, Louvre Museum

124 Honoré Daumier
Allegory of the Republic
60 × 73 cm. (24⅘" × 28¾"), 1848
Paris, Louvre Museum

125 Eugène Delacroix
Women of Algiers
229 × 180 cm. (90¼" × 71"), 1834
Paris, Louvre Museum

127 Edouard Manet
Olympia
190 × 130.5 cm. (74⅞" × 51⅖"), 1863
Paris, Jeu de Paume Museum

129 Claude Monet
Regatta at Argenteuil
73 × 48 cm. (28¾" × 19"), 1872
Paris, Jeu de Paume Museum

130 Edgar Degas
The Dance Lesson
75 × 85 cm. (29⅗" × 33½"), 1875
Paris, Louvre Museum

130 Edgar Degas
The Orchestra at the Opera
45 × 33 cm. (17¾" × 13"), 1868–69
Paris, Jeu de Paume Museum

132 Georges Seurat
High Tide at Port-en-Bressin
81 × 66 cm. (32" × 26"), 1888
Paris, Jeu de Paume Museum

132 Henri de Toulouse-Lautrec
Him, Her and the Dog
60 × 48 cm. (23⅗" × 19"), 1893
Albi, Toulouse-Lautrec Museum

132 Alfred Sisley
The Saint-Martin Canal
65 × 50 cm. (23⅗" × 19¾"), 1870
Paris, Jeu de Paume Museum

132 Paul Cézanne
Blue Vase
50 × 61 cm. (19¾" × 24"), 1883–87
Paris, Louvre Museum

132 Paul Cézanne
Card Players
57 × 45 cm. (22½" × 17¾"), 1890–92
Paris, Jeu de Paume Museum

133 Edouard Manet
Argenteuil
131 × 149 cm. (51⅗" × 58¾"), 1874
Tournai, Fine Arts Museum

133 Paul Gauguin
Haymaking in Brittany
92 × 73 cm. (36¼" × 28¾"), 1888
Paris, Louvre Museum

133 Vincent Van Gogh
Portrait of Marguerite Gachet
55 × 46 cm. (21⅔" × 18⅛"), 1890
Paris, Jeu de Paume Museum

133 Camille Pissarro
Entrance to the Village of Voisins
55 × 45 cm. (21⅔" × 17¾"), 1872
Paris, Jeu de Paume Museum

134 Vincent Van Gogh
Peasants Enjoying a Siesta
91 × 73 cm. (35⅞" × 28¾"), 1890
Paris, Jeu de Paume Museum

134 Vincent Van Gogh
Room at Arles
90 × 72 cm. (35½" × 28⅖"), 1888
Paris, Jeu de Paume Museum

135 Henri de Toulouse-Lautrec
Moorish Dance
307.5 × 285 cm. (121⅛" × 112⅓"), 1895
Paris, Jeu de Paume Museum

135 Henri de Toulouse-Lautrec
The Washerwoman
1888
Albi, Toulouse-Lautrec Museum

136 Auguste Renoir
Dance at the Moulin de la Galette
175 × 131 cm. (61" × 51⅗"), 1876
Paris, Jeu de Paume Museum

137 Auguste Renoir
Women Bathing
160 × 110 cm. (63" × 43⅓"), 1919
Paris, Jeu de Paume Museum

138 Henri Matisse
Gypsy Woman
46 × 55 cm. (18⅛" × 21⅔"), 1905–06
Saint Tropez, Musée de l'Annonciade

138 Raoul Dufy
Paddock at Deauville
130 × 54 cm. (51¼" × 21¼"), c. 1930
Paris, Georges Pompidou Museum

138 Raoul Dufy
The Red Violin
55 × 46 cm. (21⅔" × 18⅛"), 1949
Geneva, Musee d'Art et d'Histoire

139 Georges Braque
Still Life with Score by Satie
73 × 43 cm. (28¾" × 17"), 1921
Paris, Georges Pompidou Centre

139 Georges Braque
Still Life with Playing Cards
59 × 80 cm. (23¼" × 31½"), 1913
Paris, Georges Pompidou Centre

139 Fernand Léger
The Outing: Homage to Louis David
185 × 154 cm.
Paris, Georges Pompidou Centre

139 Fernand Léger
Women in a Room
65 × 54 cm. (25⅔" × 21⅓"), 1922
Paris, Georges Pompidou Centre

140 Pablo Picasso
Guernica
782.5 × 335.5 cm. (308⅛" × 132⅕"), 1937
Madrid, Prado Museum

INDEX OF NAMES

Numbers in italics refer to captions.

Picture Credits

The publisher and author wish to thank the Istituto
Fotografico Editoriale Scala of Florence, which supplied
all the photographs of the works of art reproduced
herein with the exception of the following:
page 140, Museo Nacional of Prado, Madrid
pages 64 and 116, Photographie Giraudon of Paris
page 91, the Rijksmuseum of Amsterdam

© S.P.A.D.E.M. for the works of Dufy, Léger,
Matisse and Picasso / © A.D.A.G.P. for the
works of Braque and Pissarro